The Next Step

The Next Step

A Model for Personal Discipleship

Stanley P. Johnson

RESOURCE *Publications* · Eugene, Oregon

THE NEXT STEP
A Model for Personal Discipleship

Copyright © 2014 Stanley P. Johnson. All rights reserved. Except for brief quotations in critical publications or reviews, no part of this book may be reproduced in any manner without prior written permission from the publisher. Write: Permissions. Wipf and Stock Publishers, 199 W. 8th Ave., Suite 3, Eugene, OR 97401.

Resource Publications
An Imprint of Wipf and Stock Publishers
199 W. 8th Ave., Suite 3
Eugene, OR 97401

www.wipfandstock.com

ISBN 13: 978-1-62564-736-8

Manufactured in the U.S.A.   07/07/2014

Unless otherwise identified, Scripture quotations are from The New American Standard Bible (NASB), © The Lockman Foundation 1960, 1962, 1963, 1968, 1971, 1972, 1973, 1975, 1977 and 1995.

Contents

Acknowledgments | vii

Permissions | ix

Introduction | 1

Chapter 1: Faith | 9

Chapter 2: God's Faithfulness | 20

Chapter 3: Moral Excellence | 30

Chapter 4: God as Morally Excellent | 39

Chapter 5: Knowledge | 49

Chapter 6: God as All-Knowing | 59

Chapter 7: Self-Control | 69

Chapter 8: God as All-Powerful | 79

Chapter 9: Perseverance | 89

Chapter 10: God as Sovereign | 98

Chapter 11: Godliness | 108

Chapter 12: The Holiness of God | 118

Chapter 13: Brotherly Kindness | 128

Chapter 14: God as Relational | 138

Chapter 15: Love | 148

Chapter 16: The Love of God | 158

Journaling | 167

Bibliography | 173

Acknowledgments

I would like to express my gratitude to the many people who saw me through this book; to all those who provided support, talked things over, read, wrote, and allowed me to work through its content with them and to the men who let me do a trial run with them.

I would like to thank WIPF and Stock for enabling me to publish this book and Cory Frye for his work in editing it.

Above all I want to thank my wife, Julie and the rest of my family, who supported and encouraged me to finish this project. To my son Trevor who initially helped look over its content.

I would like to thank my co-worker and Senior Pastor, Steven Cole for his comments and encouragement in this process and his message on "The Priority of True Worship."

Thanks to John Sloan for his commitment to disciple men and who designed and showed me how to use the Forum of Four verse study used in each chapter of this book.

Thanks to Pastor Tom Mercer for taking the "8 to 15" concept and modeling it to me and showing us all that the world is smaller than we think.

Thanks to Daniel Witt for showing me the value of putting together worship songs and making them a part of one's daily time with the Lord.

Permissions

Chapter 1

"Grace Greater than Our Sin" –Julia H. Johnston, Public Domain

"Only By Grace" Copyright © 1990 Integrity's Hosanna! Music (ASCAP) (adm. At CapitolCMGPublishing.com) All rights reserved. Used by permission.

Chapter 2

"Great is Thy Faithfulness" © 1923, Ren. 1951 Hope Publishing Company, Carol Stream, IL 60188. All rights reserved. Used by permission.

"Forever" Copyright © 2001 worshiptogether.com Songs (ASCAP) Sixsteps Music (ASCAP) Vamos Publishing (ASCAP) (admin. At CapitolCMGPublishing.com) All rights reserved. Used by permission.

Chapter 3

"Everlasting God" Copyright © 2005 Thankyou Music (PRS) (adm. Worldwide at CapitolCMGPublishing.com excluding Europe which is adm. by Integritymusic.com) All rights reserved. Used by permission.

"Amazing Grace" – John Newton, Public Domain

Chapter 4

"Come and See" – Author Unknown, Public Domain

"God of Wonders" Copyright © 2000 Storm Boy Music (BMI) Meaux Mercy (BMI) Never Say Never Songs (ASCAP) New Spring Publishing Inc. (ASCAP) (adm. at CapitolCMGPublishing.com) All rights reserved. Used by permission.

Chapter 5

"Sweet Hour of Prayer" – William W. Walford, Public Domain

"I Will Offer up my Life" Copyright © 1994 Thankyou Music (PRS) (adm. Worldwide at CapitolCMGPublishing.com excluding Europe which is adm. by Integritymusic.com) All rights reserved. Used by permission.

Permissions

Chapter 6

"Before There Was Time" Copyright © 2001 Stuntman Music (adm. by Music Services) All Rights Reserved. ASCAP Used by Permission.

"He Knows My Name" Copyright © 1996 Universal Music – Brentwood Benson Songs (BMI) (adm. at CapitolCMGPublishing.com) All rights reserved. Used by permission.

Chapter 7

"Only By Grace" Copyright © 1990 Integrity's Hosanna! Music (ASCAP) (adm. at CapitolCMGPublishing.com) All rights reserved. Used by permission.

"Come Thou Fount" – Robert Robinson, Public Domain

Chapter 8

"I Stand In Awe" Copyright © 2012 Sovereign Grace Praise (BMI) (adm. at CapitolCMGPublishing.com) All rights reserved. Used by permission.

"How Great Thou Art" © 1949, 1953 and this Arr. © 2013 The Stuart Hine Trust. All rights in the USA, its territories and possessions, except print rights, administered by Capitol CMG Publishing. USA, North Central and South America print rights administered by Hope Publishing Company. All other non US Americas rights administered by The Stuart Hine Trust. Rest of world rights administered by Integrity Music UK. All rights reserved. Used by permission.

Chapter 9

"It is Well with My Soul" – Horatio G. Spafford, Public Domain

"You are My Hiding Place" Copyright © 1993 Cccm Music (ASCAP) Universal Music – Brentwood Benson Publ. (ASCAP) (Adm. at CapitolCMGPublishing.com) All rights reserved. Used by permission.

Chapter 10

"Sovereign Over Us" Copyright © 2011 Thankyou Music (PRS) (adm. Worldwide at CapitolCMGPublishing.com excluding Europe which is adm. by Integritymusic.com)/worshiptogether.com Songs (ASCAP) Meaux Jeaux Music (SESAC) Jack Mooring Music (SESAC) Chief End Music (ASCAP) (adm. at CapitolCMGPublishing.com) All rights reserved. Used by permission.

"How Great Thou Art" © 1949, 1953 and this Arr. © 2013 The Stuart Hine Trust. All rights in the USA, its territories and possessions, except print rights, administered by Capitol CMG Publishing. USA, North Central and South America print rights administered by Hope Publishing Company. All other non US Americas rights administered by The Stuart Hine Trust. Rest of world rights administered by Integrity Music UK. All rights reserved. Used by permission.

Chapter 11

"I Give You My Heart" Copyright © 1995 Hillsong Music Publishing (APRA) (adm. in the US and Canada at CapitolCMGPublishing.com) All rights reserved. Used by permission.

"10,000 Reasons" Copyright © 2011 Shout! Publishing (APRA) (adm. in the US and Canada at CapitolCMGPublishing.com)/ Thankyou Music (PRS) (adm. Worldwide at

Permissions

CapitolCMGPublishing.com excluding Europe which is adm. by Integritymusic.com)/ worshiptogether.com Songs (ACAP) sixsteps Music (ASCAP) Said And Done Music (ASCAP) (adm. at CapitolCMGPublishing.com) All rights reserved. Used by permission.

Chapter 12

"Holy is the Lord" Copyright © 2003 worshiptogether.com Songs (ASCAP) sixsteps Music (ASCAP) (adm. at CapitolCMGPublishing.com) All rights reserved. Used by permission.

"Great Are You Lord" Copyright © 1984 Universal Music – Brentwood Benson Publ. (ASCAP) (adm. at CapitolCMGPublishing.com) All rights reserved. Used by permission.

Chapter 13

"O To Be Like Thee" – Thomas O. Chisholm, Public Domain

"Shout to the North" Copyright © 1995 Curious? Music UK (PRS) (adm. in the US and Canada at CapitolCMGPublishing.com) All rights reserved. Used by permission.

Chapter 14

"Amazing Love" Copyright © 1999 worshiptogether.com Songs (ASCAP) (adm. at CapitolCMGPublishing.com) All rights reserved. Used by permission.

"Whom Shall I Fear" Copyright © 2013 Worship Together Music (BMI) Sixsteps Songs (BMI) A Thousand Generations Publ. (BMI) (adm. at CapitolCMGPublishing.com)/ ***NEW ALLETROP*** (BMI)/ C/O MUSIC SERVICES (BMI) All rights reserved. Used by permission.

Chapter 15

"The Heart of Worship" Copyright © 1999 Thankyou Music (PRS) (adm. Worldwide at CapitolCMGPublishing.com excluding Europe which is adm. by Inegritymusic.com) All rights reserved. Used by permission.

"I Could Sing of Your Love Forever" Copyright © 1994 Curious? Music UK (PRS) (adm. in the US and Canada at CapitolCMGPublishing.com) All rights reserved. Used by permission.

Chapter 16

"My Savior's Love" – Charles H. Gabriel, Public Domain

"Your Love Never Fails" Copyright © 1999 Thankyou Music (PRS) (adm. worldwide at CapitolCMGPublishing.com excluding Europe which is adm. by Integritymusic.com) All rights reserved. Used by permission.

Introduction

One of the principles Patrick Morley gives for ministering to the men in your church in *No Man Left Behind* is that whenever you plan an event or activity for men, keep your momentum, "always have a right next step."[1] This is why I have titled this book *The Next Step*. As someone comes to know Jesus Christ as his or her Savior and Lord, what is the next step? If someone has been a believer for a while and wants to grow, what is the next step? If someone has grown in his or her faith and wants to know how to help another believer grow, what is the next step? This book will begin to answer that question.

By way of introduction, here are some *reasons for putting together this discipleship tool*, some examples of *how to use it*, and finally, *highlights of some of this study's unique features* that I hope will become part of your daily walk with God.

Why I wrote this discipleship tool

I grew up on a peach farm in the central valley of California. There, I was able to see firsthand what went into developing a productive orchard. You need the following ingredients: regular fertilizer, regular watering, weed control, pruning, thinning, propping of branches as the peaches ripened, and harvesting. All of these were necessary to produce healthy trees and a good fruit crop. If you left out any of these parts, you didn't have healthy peach trees or, possibly, any fruit at all.

In the same way that more than one chore or task goes into growing good peaches, we grow best in our relationship with God as we give attention to what He wants us to grow in. Studying scripture, I observe that I am

1. Morely, *No Man Left Behind*, 151.

The Next Step

to grow in *Knowledge, Character* and *Ministry Skills*. As I read and study 2 Peter 1, three principles especially stand out:

Knowledge is an essential foundation for character growth. Peter writes in verses 2 through 4, "Grace and peace be multiplied to you in the knowledge of God and of Jesus our Lord; seeing that His divine power has granted to us everything pertaining to life and godliness, through the true knowledge of Him who called us by His own glory and excellence. For by these He has granted to us His precious and magnificent promises, so that by them you may become partakers of the divine nature, having escaped the corruption that is in the world by lust."

Character growth is critical for being complete in Christ. Peter continues in 2 Peter 1, verse 5: "Now, for this very reason also, applying all diligence, in your faith supply moral excellence, and in your moral excellence, knowledge, and in your knowledge, self-control, and in your self-control, perseverance, and in your perseverance, godliness, and in your godliness, brotherly kindness, and in your brotherly kindness, love."

Service or ministry is essential in the character-building process and is also a natural byproduct. Peter writes about the fruit of our growing faith in verses 8 through 11, giving us the promise of fruitful and useful lives: "For if these qualities are yours and are increasing, they render you neither useless nor unfruitful in the true knowledge of our Lord Jesus Christ."

In Ephesians 4: 11–16, Paul points out that as we use our gifts in serving one another, we grow individually and as a church body:

> And He gave some as apostles, and some as prophets, and some as evangelists, and some as pastors and teachers, for the equipping of the saints for the work of service, to the building up of the body of Christ; until we all attain to the unity of the faith, and of the knowledge of the Son of God, to a mature man, to the measure of the stature which belongs to the fullness of Christ. As a result, we are no longer to be children, tossed here and there by waves and carried about by every wind of doctrine, by the trickery of men, by craftiness in deceitful scheming; but speaking the truth in love, we are to grow up in all aspects into Him who is the head, even Christ, from whom the whole body, being fitted and held together by what every joint supplies, according to the proper working of each individual part, causes the growth of the body for the building up of itself in love.

Another way to look at this is to see where we lack when one of these three are missing.

Introduction

- If I am strong in knowledge and service but lack in Christlike character, then I disqualify myself for service and am a stumbling block for other Christians. (See I Corinthians 9:27 and 2 Timothy 2:20–23.)
- If I am strong in character and service but lack in knowledge, then I am a weak Christian and can easily be led astray from my faith. (See Colossians 2:8 and 1 Timothy 6:20–21.)
- If I am strong in character and knowledge but lack in service and ministry, then I am a fat and lazy believer. I'm not exercising my faith and putting it into practice. In fact, I am fooling myself. (See Joshua 1:8 and James 1:21–25.)

Note: We're probably never strong in one and totally absent in the other two, but often we are weak in one or two of these.

One of the reasons I wanted to develop this study was to help a believer grow in each of these: Knowledge, Character and Ministry. I wanted to do this in such a way as to mix these three throughout this study.

A second reason that I put this study together was to present a set of material to use in discipling someone. During a recent meeting with some of the men in our church, we were studying "The Trellis and the Vine." This book, by Colin Marshall and Tony Payne, tackles the balance between programs in the church and ministry to people. A discussion near the end of Chapter 1 shows the book's emphasis.

> "Thus the goal of Christian ministry is quite simple, and in a sense measurable: are we making and nurturing genuine disciples of Christ? The church always tends towards institutionalism and secularization. The focus shifts to preserving traditional programs and structures, and the goal of discipleship is lost. The mandate of disciple-making provides the touchstone for whether our church is engaging in Christ's mission. Are we making genuine disciples of Jesus Christ? Our goal is not to make church members or members of our institution, but genuine disciples of Jesus." [2]

In our discussion, we talked about how we could emphasize to more of our men to be discipled and to disciple others. One of the main needs identified in that discussion was material to use in discipling another person. I hope this is the beginning of developing that material. This workbook is designed in such a way that someone could take it and be prepared for

---

2. Marshall and Payne, *Trellis*, 14.

two or more people to go through together. At the end of this introduction I will present more models of how this material can be used.

A third reason for developing this material and in this format is to create within us a passion to know Christ and make Him known. Two verses that express my desire for those who work through this book are Hebrews 12:2: "Fixing our eyes on Jesus the author and perfecter of faith," and James 4:8: "Draw near to God and He will draw near to you."

We each have the privilege of growing intimately in our daily relationship with God as Enoch "walked with God" (Genesis 5:22 & 24). God also desires to use us in helping others walk closely with Him. God's method of ministry is people-to-people. Along that line, in each chapter are boxes with principles to help one as a growing disciple as well as principles to help someone disciple another.

A fourth reason for writing this material is to offer a plan and model to every believer who doesn't want to waste the rest of his or her life. God has a plan and desire for your life and it begins by growing in your relationship with Him. Working in churches over the past three decades, I've seen many men and women who have been in church for years and involved in various Bible studies and home fellowships. Many of these people are not involved in an ongoing ministry and seem unable to "find" a ministry. Investing your life in other men and women is a very worthwhile ministry, one in which, I believe, everyone can take part. This study will help start a person in a ministry he or she will use the rest of his or her life.

A final reason for putting this material together in this format, and probably the beginning reason, *was to help myself grow in knowledge, character, and ministry skills.* God has often brought me back to 2 Peter over the past few years. In doing so I have been reminded how much I fall short of seeing these seven character qualities in my life. But God always reminds me of this with clarity and grace. I pray that God will use this "project" in my life to help me grow closer to Him and more like Him.

By intermingling character qualities with knowledge about God, spiritual disciplines and ministry skills, we do "things" out of our relationship with our heavenly Father. I hope you and I will see the privilege of "spiritual disciplines" as opportunities to spend more time with our heavenly Father, who desires fellowship with us. James 4:5 is a verse that has fascinated me lately: "Or do you think that the Scripture speaks to no purpose: 'He jealously desires the Spirit which He has made to dwell in us'?" God jealously wants to live in us. He wants that relationship. Do you?

Introduction

How to use this discipleship tool

Here are five ways you can use this study; you might come up with more.

1. You can use this workbook by yourself in your daily walk with God. Pick a time of day that's good for you, a time when you're alert and have the least amount of distractions. Mornings work well for some, but it can be anytime. The key here is to make it regular. Consider it a daily appointment with the Lord. Then get started, working through one chapter each week.

2. You can use this workbook with a friend (your spouse or another believer) to work on personally during the week and then pick a weekly time to meet and share what God has taught you. (See #1 for ideas on your personal time working through it.)

3. You can use this workbook as a tool to disciple another believer. Go over how to work through a chapter each week and then plan a time to meet and interact on what you've both learned. Be flexible enough to spend extra time on areas he or she has questions about.

4. You can use this workbook in a small group to grow together. I've included some discussion questions at the end of each chapter.

5. You can use this workbook to help train your children to be fully devoted followers of Christ. Just be careful to not pressure them in this. Work through the material together and at their pace.

Note: Let me encourage you to spread out your reading and study time as much as possible over a whole week. The advantage of doing some daily reading and studying is that it will help develop the habit of a daily walk with the Lord. (Again, remember God's grace here. We all have different and busy schedules, so use my recommendations as suggestions. As the Lord gives you time, enjoy working through these chapters with His guidance.)

Highlights of some unique features in this Study

- *Spiritual Disciplines* — Three spiritual disciplines are addressed and encouraged in this book: *A Daily Quiet Time, Scripture Memory* and *Journaling*.

The Next Step

As to the *Quiet Time*, I'm encouraging you to spread your study over a whole week and pick the same time each day, if possible. If you do this for 16 weeks, this will help develop the habit of a daily quiet time with the Lord.

In each chapter is a key verse you can memorize and do verse studies for. By memorizing these verses you will be doing an informal study by thinking a lot about their details. I find that the process of memorizing a verse causes me to ask why certain words were used and how the ideas in a verse fit together. In Scripture Memory, you are handing tools to the Holy Spirit that He will use in your life.

For *Journaling*, my goal here is to provide the opportunity to spend a little time every day to "journal," or write down what you learn from the Lord. Part of the goal here is to help develop a daily Quiet Time. Another reason for journaling is that we think through ideas a little further if we take the time to process what we're learning and write it down.

- *Grace* — I am introducing several new things in this workbook, and I hope you take full advantage of them. In every chapter I hope to deal with both spiritual discipline and grace. Paul states in I Corinthians 15:10: "But by the grace of God I am what I am, and His grace toward me did not prove vain; but I labored even more than all of them, yet not I, but the grace of God with me."

Paul often talked about exerting a lot of effort in growing as a believer and in serving the Lord, and he always talked about grace. The verse probably quoted the most to promote discipleship is 2 Timothy 2:2: "The things which you have heard from me in the presence of many witnesses, entrust these to faithful men who will be able to teach others also." In the previous verse, Paul states, "You therefore, my son, be strong in the grace that is in Christ Jesus." I think Paul was telling Timothy to get all the grace from God that he could, and also, freely give grace to others.

Therefore, I hope to look at grace in every chapter and especially as we examine some wonderful spiritual disciplines, or opportunities to grow in our relationship with our Savior.

- Personal Worship — Another area I want to introduce weekly is personal worship. In an Aug. 11, 2013, message titled "The Priority of True Worship," Pastor Steve Cole said, "It's no accident that the longest book in the Bible, Psalms, is all about praising and worshiping God. When we get to the end of the Bible, we see the saints and angels in heaven falling on their faces and worshiping God (Rev. 4:10-11; 5:8-14; 7:9-11). Since worship will be our ceaseless activity and greatest

Introduction

joy in heaven, we ought to be practicing it now."[3] When you look at King David in the Old Testament, we see worship as one of the factors that made him a man after God's own heart.

The idea here is to include in one's daily quiet time a time of worship and praise to God. We are told that worshipping God is more than just the 20 to 30 minutes each week that we sing praise songs before the message, yet in practice that is what we think. I have a good friend at Flagstaff Christian Fellowship who collects songs from old hymn books and chorus sheets from what we sing at the church. He's put these together to make his own praise book and uses them in his daily quiet time. I will be introducing a praise song each week for you to sing or just meditate upon as part of your daily time with the Lord. You will be amazed at the encouragement it gives you and how it helps us "fix our eyes on Jesus."

- *Ministry Skill: "8 to 15"* — A fourth idea or area I want to give you in each chapter is the idea of "8 to 15," or thinking through and praying for the 8 to 15 people God has recently brought into your life. Tom Mercer, a pastor at High Desert Church in Victorville, California, presented "8 to 15" to a group of us at a pastor's conference in 2011.[4] He introduced this as one of the simplest yet most profound tools to help us reach out to the people God put into our lives. I will be giving you some of his encouragement and insights throughout this study.

Sometimes, when we are taught how to be Christ's disciples, our growth as a believer and our "commission" to share our faith are separated. Also, the idea of "witnessing" is presented as a difficult task to test our boldness for Christ. I do not want to ignore the fact that we need boldness, and fear does exist as we think about speaking out about Christ, but these are not the main ideas related to sharing our faith. As we study character qualities and knowledge about God and ministry skills each week, we will look at how God has put people into our lives. By starting with daily prayer for them, God will do some amazing things in their lives as we pray for them and as we see God use us.

- *Life Principles* — The fifth idea I have added to this workbook is life principles. These will be highlighted in boxes, some to help you as a growing disciple of Christ and others to guide you in discipling another. My desire in preparing this workbook is not only that you and I

---

3. Cole, "True Worship."
4. Mercer, *8 to 15*.

would grow in our daily walk with the Lord, but that we would in turn entrust or give this to other faithful men and women so they can learn from it and pass it on to others. That is discipleship, and we all have the privilege to be part of it.

> Life Principle: Everything God gives us is to equip us to be more generous to others. "And God is able to make all grace abound to you, so that always having all sufficiency in everything, you may have an abundance for every good deed (including all He teaches us)" (2 Corinthians 9:8).

Chapter 1

Faith

Our study focuses on Peter's second letter, and especially the character qualities we are to supply or add to our faith. Peter was one of the 12 apostles Christ asked to follow Him. He was also one of the three disciples who spent a lot of personal time with Christ. Peter was given several opportunities to exercise faith and to grow in faith. One of those occasions is recorded in Matthew 14:22–33. Early in the morning, while the disciples were crossing the Sea of Galilee, Christ "came to them, walking on the sea" (Matthew 14:25). The disciple's response was at first fear, but when they hear the Lord's voice, their fears were calmed and Peter said, "Lord, if it is you, command me to come to you on the water." Peter began to walk to Christ on the water, but as he looked at the waves he began to be afraid and sink. Christ took his hand and Peter stepped into the boat. This was a lesson on faith and how Christ needs to be the focus of our faith. Peter would never forget it. I will be giving you more information on Peter as we work through this book.

The letter of 2 Peter is his second letter we have recorded, sent to scattered believers throughout the North Eastern Mediterranean sea. In this letter Peter addressed the development or growth of our faith, the danger of false teachers, the assurance of God's judgment of the unrighteous and the assurance of God's preservation of the righteous.

The core of Peter's teaching on the development of our faith is found in 2 Peter 1:5–7 and will provide the outline of this study:

> Now for this very reason also, applying all diligence, in your faith
> supply moral excellence, and in your moral excellence, knowledge,

and in your knowledge, self-control, and in your self-control, perseverance, and in your perseverance, godliness, and in your godliness, brotherly kindness, and in your brotherly kindness, love.

Peter begins this list by writing in verse 5, "in your *faith* supply moral excellence," etc. Since Peter begins with faith, we will study this faith in our first chapter. I will also be introducing you more to segments on *Journaling, How to Study a Verse, What about Grace?, Ministry Skills*, and the place of *Personal Worship*.

Start your time with the Lord in prayer. Here's an example I use as I reflect on these verses, praying either all or part of these requests:

- "Lord, as I begin a new day that you've given me, help me to fix my eyes on you, the author and perfecter of my faith." (Hebrews 12:2)
- "Lord, by your grace and mercy, forgive my sin and cleanse my heart" (Psalm 51:1-4, 10-13). "Please help me, in humility, receive your word to grow and do its work in me." (James 1:21)
- "Lord, help me put into action what you show me (James 1:22), and help me see the opportunities you give me to share something of encouragement to someone else today" (2 Timothy 2:2 & Ephesians 4:29).
- "Lord, I want to worship you today, so help me do that, (Romans 12:1,2 & Psalm 8) and help me to be strong in your grace to experience it and to share it" (2 Timothy 2:1). "And help my satisfaction and delight be in you today" (Psalm 34:8 & 37:4).

> *To the Disciple and Discipler*: The greatest impact you can have on anyone is through prayer, for in prayer we bring in God and all of His attributes, wisdom and resources.

Now, read Psalm 62:1-8 and write down something to thank the Lord for.

Next, write Ephesians 2:8 and 9 onto a 3-by-5 card and read it several times. Plan to carry it with you this week.

Faith

Journaling

At the end of this book I've included some pages for journaling. Periodically, I like to write down on a daily or weekly basis what God has been teaching me in my daily quiet time. Turn to the back section on journaling and you'll see an explanation and pages where you may write about what God is teaching you and how you can respond to Him accordingly.

Journaling is not an assignment to be turned in. Rather, it's a tool to help us interact a little more with God and His word. When I was in seminary, a professor shared with my class that a pencil and notepad are great tools to help us engage with the content of God's word. The places in this workbook for journaling are opportunities to engage in more depth with the Lord.

How to Study a Verse of the Bible

Next, I would like to introduce to you how to study a Bible verse. We will be using this during each chapter. This will also provide you with a useful tool in the future as you continue to study the Bible. In this first chapter, I will give you more of an explanation for each part of the verse analysis.

> To the Disciple: "In humility receive the word implanted," from James 1:21, reminds me to always recognize my weaknesses and need for God to perform a daily miracle in my life. Often pray, "Lord, I need you today!" Humility speaks to how I come to God, asking for His grace.

Forum Verse Analysis[1]

Verse: Ephesians 2:8, 9

Context:
    Who is speaking? Who is the audience? What is the subject? What is the time frame, beginning and ending thought?

---

1. Sloan, "Forums of Four."

The Next Step

Key Words:

Pick out the key words and define them. In light of the definitions, how do they expand or highlight this verse for me? (Define using *Vines*, *Strong's Concordance*, or English dictionary)

Cross References:

Verses that support my understanding of this verse, or help in understanding this verse

For Discussion

- What is the main issue being addressed here?

- What about this verse is challenging for me to believe? (What are the implications for my thinking?)

- What sinful thinking or behavior does this verse expose in me? (What are the implications for my living life?)

Faith

- What would applying this truth in my life look like?

- How can we encourage one another in the truth of this verse?

Write this verse on a 3-by-5 card and carry it with you. As you have breaks during the day, take the time to look over this verse and contemplate its meaning while thinking through the above questions.

> To the Discipler: Fill all the blanks and complete this study yourself. You want to share fresh what God is teaching you and be up on all the points in each study. However, be sure to allow those you are discipling to experience the joy of discovery.

Let's further examine Faith, beginning with Peter's opening comment in 2 Peter 1:1: "Simon Peter, a bondservant and apostle of Jesus Christ, to those who have received *a faith of the same kind as ours*, by the righteousness of our God and Savior, Jesus Christ."

What is this faith Peter is talking about? He's talking about trusting in what Christ did for me on the cross. As the above verse explains, this faith is "by the righteousness of our God and Savior, Jesus Christ." It's His righteousness that saves us, not ours. He is talking about Christ accomplishing something I could not. This is called "saving faith."

This kind of faith is not a momentary faith, as when I ask God to keep my family safe, or when I ask God to help me pass a test. While that is a type of faith, it's not what Peter is talking about here.

Also, this kind of faith is not just academic, like when my teacher in grade school taught us about George Washington or Abraham Lincoln. I had a kind of faith in what she told us, but that was intellectual faith, not saving faith.

The Next Step

James Kennedy explained it well. Saving faith is believing that Christ "died on the cross to pay the penalty for our sins and rose from the grave to purchase a place in heaven for us. Jesus Christ bore our sin in His body on the cross and now offers you eternal life (heaven) as a free gift. This gift is received by Faith. Saving Faith is trusting in Jesus Christ alone for eternal life. It means resting upon Christ alone and what He has done rather than in what you or I have done to get us into heaven."[2]

This is the faith Peter talks about in verse 5, to which we are to supply the following seven character qualities. Let me ask you a question I've found very helpful in discerning how well someone understands saving faith. If you were to die tonight and stand before God and He asked you "Why should I let you into my heaven?"[3] What would you say? *Take a few minutes to think about your answer and then write it here*:

If your answer includes anything about things you have done to earn heaven, then you don't understand saving faith or grace. Eternal life is a free gift. We can't earn it, and we don't deserve it. It's given by a gracious God, and our part is to believe what He said about our need of a savior to forgive us our sins, to ask for forgiveness and then to receive that gift by trusting in what Christ did on the cross for us.

The character qualities we will be studying are to be supplied to this kind of faith. In the same way that grace was involved in our salvation, it is also involved in our daily growth as believers.

What about grace?

You've already been introduced to grace in our key verse, Ephesians 2:8, 9, and it should have been one of the key words you looked up and defined. Each week we'll look at God's grace and how it relates to that week's topic. Another way of saying this is that we will look at how God's compassion and generosity, which we have not earned, are part of the character qualities

---

2. Kennedy, "Do You Know."
3. Ibid.

Faith

integral to growth. Grace is part of everything known about God and is very involved in every way we serve Him and each other.

As we look at saving faith, it will be helpful to see a definition of Grace. "Grace is the generous overflow of the love of God the Father toward the Son, Jesus Christ. This love is most clearly demonstrated to humans through God's selfless giving of Jesus to enable people to enter into a loving relationship with God as the Holy Spirit enables them. Efficacious grace refers to the special application of grace to a person who comes by faith to Christ for salvation."[4] In *Systematic Theology*, Wayne Grudem defines grace as "God's goodness toward those who deserve only punishment."[5]

Therefore, as I understand God's grace in bringing me to Himself and saving me, I am tremendously grateful for His gift of grace. All my works that follow are an expression of gratitude and not done to "pay back" what I have received by His grace.

As we have looked at saving faith, it is by God's grace that we can have this faith.

Ministry Skills: "8 to 15"

As mentioned in the introduction, one of this study's unique features is to pray every week for the 8 to 15 people God has put in your life. Tom Mercer introduced me to this simple tool. This is how he describes this tool, or model, of how the early church grew:

> On average, each of us has 8 to 15 people, whom God has supernaturally and strategically placed in our relational world so that He might use us to show them His love. The Greeks used one word to describe this personal world—OIKOS, or "extended household." OIKOS is not a program. It's not an event. It's not an emphasis. The oikos principle is the heartbeat of Christ's Church. Jesus designed it, modeled it and taught us how to use it.[6]

In this part of our study, you will begin to identify the 8 to 15 people God has supernaturally placed in your life and pray for them daily. Each week I will give you a little more input on what to do with your list. For the first week, take some time to ask God to open your eyes and begin

---

4. Grenz et al, *Pocket Dictionary*, 56.
5. Grudem, *Systematic Theology*, 1243.
6. Mercer, *8 to 15*, back cover.

The Next Step

adding names. Do you have coworkers, friends, neighbors or relatives who are unchurched?

List your 8 to 15:

1.

2.

3.

4.

5.

6.

7.

8.

9.

10.

11.

12.

13.

14.

15.

Personal Worship

As mentioned in the introduction, worship and praise songs will be included in every chapter to help us spend some time praising the Lord. (This can be done quietly, loudly or silently, as the tastes of those around you allow.) I have very much enjoyed the times I have taken, apart from a Sunday morning service, to praise the Lord in song, but I don't do this very often. I'm including this in this workbook because I want to grow in daily praising the Lord.

I will give you two worship songs or praise choruses in each chapter, but feel free to look for ones that you feel are fitting responses to the content. I also hope this will become a regular habit in your daily *Quiet Time*.

For growing in and understanding our "Faith" which we have because of God's grace, I've included these songs:

"Grace Greater Than Our Sin"

Marvelous Grace of our loving Lord,
Grace that exceeds our sin and our guilt!
Yonder on Calvary's mount outpoured
There where the blood of the lamb was spilt.
(Chorus)
Grace, grace, God's grace,
Grace that will pardon and cleanse within;
Grace, grace, God's grace,
Grace that is greater than all our sin!

Sin and despair, like the sea waves cold,
Threaten the soul with infinite loss;
Grace that is greater yes, grace untold
Points to the refuge the mighty cross.

Dark is the stain that we cannot hide,
What can avail to wash it away?
Look! There is flowing a crimson tide;
Whiter than snow you may be today.

Marvelous, infinite, matchless grace,
Freely bestowed on all who believe!
You that are longing to see His face,
Will you this moment His grace receive?[7]

"Only By Grace"

Only by grace can we enter, Only by grace can we stand
Not by our human endeavor, But by the blood of the Lamb

Into Your presence You call us, You call us to come
Into Your presence You draw us, And now by Your grace we come

Lord, if You mark our transgressions Who would stand
Thanks to Your grace we are cleansed By the blood of the Lamb

7. Julia H. Johnston, Public Domain.

The Next Step

> Lord, if You mark our transgressions Who would stand
> Thanks to Your grace we are cleansed
> By the blood of the Lamb[8]

Consider This: (For Group discussion)

1. What are some of the ways you exercise faith in your daily life?

2. Review what God taught you as you worked through the verse study on Ephesians 2:8 and 9.

3. What was a highlight of this chapter on faith?

4. What kind of faith do you have? Is it a saving faith? How do you know?

5. How is faith a gift?

---

8. Gerrit Gustafson (Integrity's Hosanna! Music, 1990).

Faith

6. As you reflect on this chapter, is there a response that God desires from you?

Chapter 2

God's Faithfulness

In the first week, we looked at Faith as the foundation for which we supply seven virtues or character qualities. This week we will look at and study God's faithfulness. Part of growing in our faith is to understand the object of our faith and how very faithful He is.

Start your time with the Lord in prayer. Here's the example I gave you in chapter 1:

- "Lord, as I begin a new day that you've given me, help me to fix my eyes on you, the author and perfecter of my faith" (Hebrews 12:2).
- "Lord, by your grace and mercy, forgive my sin and cleanse my heart" (Psalm 51:1-4, 10-13). Please help me, in humility, receive your word to grow and do its work in me" (James 1:21).
- "Lord, help me put into action what you show me (James 1:22), and help me see the opportunities you give me to share something of encouragement to someone else today" (2 Timothy 2:2 & Ephesians 4:29).
- "Lord, I want to worship you today, so help me do that (Romans 12:1,2 & Psalm 8), and help me to be strong in your grace to experience it and to share it" (2 Timothy 2:1). "And help my satisfaction and delight be in you today" (Psalm 34:8 & 37:4).

> To the Disciple: A life principle that also relates to God's faithfulness is: "God's provision for our need always begins with prayer."

God's Faithfulness

Now, read Psalm 119:89–96 and Psalm 89:1, 2, and write down something for which to thank the Lord.

Next, copy Lamentations 3:22,23 onto a 3-by-5 card and read it several times. Plan to carry it with you this week along with your Ephesians 2:8 and 9 card. If you read this verse several times a day last week, you should begin to know it by memory. Keep working on memorizing both of these verses and review them daily. A memorized verse is like a tool you hand to God that He can use in your life at any time. Time will show the tremendous value of this.

Journaling

As you have opportunity this week, write down in the Journaling section something God has taught you from these two memory verses and this study, and respond to God with a prayer.

> To the Discipler: Be honest and vulnerable with those you are discipling. You will earn their trust as they get to know you and see that you share honestly from your heart.

Verse Study

As you begin to study Lamentations 3:22 and 23, look at not only the individual words but the phrases in this wonderful promise.

Forum Verse Analysis

Verse:

Lamentations 3:22 and 23

The Next Step

Context:

Who is speaking? Who is the audience? What is the subject? What is the time frame, beginning and ending thought?

Key Words:

In light of the definitions, how do they expand or highlight this verse for me?

Cross References:

Verses that support my understanding of this verse

For Discussion:

- What is the main issue being addressed here?

- What about this verse is challenging for me to believe?

- What sinful thinking or behavior does this verse expose in me?

- What would applying this truth in my life look like?

- How can we encourage one another in the truth of this verse?

Let's further examine God's faithfulness by answering three questions.
1. What does God's faithfulness mean?

"God's faithfulness means that God will always do what He has said and fulfill what He has promised."[1] We read in Numbers 23:19, "God is not a man that He should lie, nor a son of man, that He should repent; has He said and will He not do it? Or has He spoken, and will He not make it good?"

The faithfulness of God means that in God's very nature, what He says is true and His actions will always be consistent with His truth and what He says.

One sense of God's faithfulness is that He is truthful. What He says and promises is based on truth. What He says and promises comes from His character of truthfulness. Another sense of God's faithfulness is that He never changes. He is consistent and unchanging.

2. What are the implications to us as believers, of God's faithfulness?

When God says something in His word, we can trust Him to always be faithful to this. Saying that God is faithful, means that He is trustworthy. We can trust what He says and know He will never be unfaithful to those who trust in Him.

---

1. Grudem, *Systematic Theology*, 195.

The Next Step

The following illustration shows how the object of our faith is critical to the results of exercising our faith, as this illustration points out. We need enough faith to act, but it's the object of our faith that is key to the outcome. Since God is the object of our faith, He and His character are most critical.[2]

It is also important to address other attributes of God when looking at His faithfulness. Implied in looking at God's faithfulness and truthfulness is His ability to do anything He says He can do; therefore, we recognize Him being all-powerful and all-knowing. If God didn't have the ability to accomplish what He promises, He would not be faithful or truthful because He would be promising something He could not fulfill. The rest of His attributes are similarly important as they relate to His ability and trustworthiness. In the midst of the prophet Jeremiah looking to God for deliverance and compassion, Jeremiah reminds himself and the people of Israel that God is all-powerful (Jeremiah 32:16-27).

3. How can I respond to God's faithfulness?

The author of Hebrews tells us in 10:23, "Let us hold fast the confession of our hope without wavering, for He who promised is faithful." We can hold fast to the hope we have in Christ because of God's faithfulness. As you regularly spend time reading and meditating on God's word, let God and what He says be a rock to help you stand firm. In a world where we

---

2. From the Navigators' "Design for Discipleship" study series, #3.

hope those with whom we work keep their word, we can have confidence that God will!

What about grace?

It is because of God's grace that we can experience His faithfulness. This is not something we have earned or deserve. An Old Testament synonym to grace is compassion. In the memory verses for the week, Lamentations 3:22 and 23, we were reminded that "The Lord's lovingkindnesses indeed never cease, for His compassions never fail. They are new every morning; great is Your faithfulness." The author here connects God's compassion (or grace) with His faithfulness. God will always be faithful, partly because He will never run out of compassion.

We see another aspect of God's grace toward us in delivering us from our temptations. In I Corinthians 10:13, Paul writes, "No temptation has overtaken you but such as is common to man; and God is faithful, who will not allow you to be tempted beyond what you are able, but with the temptation will provide the way of escape also, so that you will be able to endure it." God has every right to leave me to wrestle through my temptations, but He knows that I am weak and that if allowed, some temptations will overwhelm me. In His grace, He will not let me be tempted beyond what I can resist by His strength, and He promises to help me endure. That's grace.

Ministry Skills: "8 to 15"

How's your "8 to 15" list coming along? It will take a little time to make this a habit. I asked this question on the Internet, "How long does it take to create a habit?" I received this answer from Ask: "Studies have shown that it takes about three weeks for people to develop a habit, or break old ones. Everyone is different, but at three weeks the new habit will become easier and more welcome." Now, this is just one person's opinion, but I find from experience that this is pretty close.

I think part of the reason we give the necessary effort to establish a new habit is related to the potential significance of that "habit." In establishing the habit of praying for your 8 to 15, you will see lives changed and God will use you to see some of those come to saving faith in Christ. That is significant!

The Next Step

As you work through this study, let me encourage you to set aside a particular time each day to establish the habit of daily listening to God from His word and responding to Him in prayer, including prayer for those "8 to 15." Part of your initial prayer might be "Who, Lord, should I put on my list?" Pray that prayer and He will be faithful to answer it. This time, as you list your 8 to 15, can you write something you have learned about each person? For confidentiality purposes you might want to jot those notes on another piece of paper.

List your 8 to 15:

1.

2.

3.

4.

5.

6.

7.

8.

9.

10.

11.

12.

13.

14.

15.

Personal Worship

Here are two more songs to help us spend some time praising the Lord. I found this quote by John MacArthur helpful as we think about praise and worship: "Worship, by the way, is not music. Worship is loving God. Worship is honoring God. Worship is knowing God for who He is, adoring Him, obeying Him, proclaiming Him as a way of life. Music is one way we express that adoration."[3] I have included some worship songs, even though worship is much more than singing, because they can stay with us throughout the day. Feel free to take these with you to further reflect on God's faithfulness through song.

Again, feel free to look for ones you feel are fitting responses to this chapter's content. I also hope this will become a regular habit in your daily quiet time.

For growing in and understanding God's faithfulness, I've included these songs:

"Great Is Thy Faithfulness"

Great is Thy faithfulness, O God my Father!
There is no shadow of turning with Thee;
Thou changest not, Thy compassions, they fail not:
As Thou hast been Thou forever wilt be.

Great is Thy faithfulness, Great is Thy faithfulness,
Morning by morning new mercies I see;
All I have needed Thy hand hath provided,
Great is Thy faithfulness, Lord, unto me!

Summer and winter, and springtime and harvest,
Sun, moon, and stars in their courses above,
Join with all nature in manifold witness
To Thy great faithfulness, mercy, and love.
Pardon for sin and a peace that endureth,
Thine own dear presence to cheer and to guide,
Strength for today and bright hope for tomorrow,
Blessings all mine, with ten thousand beside![4]

---

3. Cole, "True Worship," 2.

4. Thomas O. Chisholm, William M. Runyan (Hope Publishing Company, Renewal 1951).

The Next Step

"Forever"

Give thanks to the Lord our God and King
His love endures forever
For He is good, He is above all things
His love endures forever
Sing praise, sing praise

With a mighty hand and outstretched arm
His love endures forever
For the life that's been reborn, His love endures forever
Sing praise, sing praise

Forever God is faithful, Forever God is strong
Forever God is with us, Forever

From the rising to the setting sun His love endures forever
By the grace of God we will carry on His love endures forever
Sing praise, sing praise[5]

Consider This: (For Group discussion)

1. What did God teach you as you studied Lamentations 3:22 and 23?

2. Share a key point you learned from this chapter on God's faithfulness.

3. How is the idea of "a new start" refreshing and encouraging to you?

---

5. Chris Tomlin (River Music Songs/Sixsteps Publishing, 2000).

God's Faithfulness

4. Try to identify one way God has shown you His faithfulness.

5. Is God showing you 8 to 15 people He has put in your life? How has God put them there?

6. Who can you share with about God's lovingkindness shown to you?

Chapter 3

Moral Excellence

During our first week, we looked at Faith as the foundation for our seven virtues or character qualities. Last week we looked at the One we can confidently put our faith in, and His faithfulness. This week we will look at the first character quality we are to add to our faith: Moral Excellence. "Now for this very reason also, applying all diligence, in your *faith* supply *moral excellence*" (2 Peter 1:5a).

Start your time with the Lord in prayer. You can refer to the examples I gave you on page 13. Another great prayer to begin the day with is from Psalm 139:23 and 24:

> "Search me, O God, and know my heart; try me and know my anxious thoughts; and see if there be any hurtful way in me, and lead me in the everlasting way."

> To the Disciple: Remember that God sees your heart as clearly as you or I see each other's face. ". . . for the Lord searches all hearts, and understands every intent of the thoughts" (1 Chronicles 28:9).

Now, read Isaiah 42:8–12 and write something praise-worthy about God:

Moral Excellence

Copy Joshua 1:9 onto a 3-by-5 card and read it several times. Keep it with your first two cards and review them now. Keep working on memorizing these verses and review them daily. Keep handing the Holy Spirit these tools to use in your life.

> To the Discipler: Spend some time talking with those you meet about these verses and what you do to help yourself memorize scripture. The key to getting verses down well is the daily review. *A verse reviewed every day for 6 weeks will stay with you your whole life.*

Journaling

Go to the end of this book and enter something in the Journaling section about what God has taught you from these memory verses and respond to God with a prayer.

Verse Study

Now work through the following study with Joshua 1:9. As you carry your 3-by-5 cards look for downtimes — waiting in a line or in between meetings and appointments — to review them.

> To the Disciple: By spreading your reading and studying over several days, you add a lot of "thinking" time in between your official study time. That's what meditating means: You're contemplating the ideas God is giving you from scripture.

Verse: Joshua 1:9

Context:

Who is speaking? Who is the audience? What is the subject? What is the time frame, beginning and ending thought?

The Next Step

Key Words:

In light of the definitions, how do they expand or highlight this verse for me?

Cross References:

Verses that support my understanding of this verse.

For Discussion:

- What is the main issue being addressed here?

- What about this verse is challenging for me to believe?

- What sinful thinking or behavior does this verse expose in me?

Moral Excellence

- What would applying this truth in my life look like?

- How can we encourage one another in the truth of this verse?

In this chapter we're studying the first character quality we supply to our faith: *Moral Excellence*. The Greek word used in 2 Peter 1:5 for "moral excellence" is *arĕte*. *Arĕte* can be defined as strength of character with moral implications. *Arĕte* combines the qualities of strength to act and being morally upright. In New Testament times it was the strength to do the right thing in the eyes of God. By saying there was a moral foundation to this quality meant the person always acted morally upright before God.

"I have the Godly courage and resolution to do the right thing." It is important to include courage and resolution. Arĕte *involves both strength and will to act. A person described by this word lived by Godly convictions. They have a moral power or energy, "vigor of soul."*[1]

In the Old Testament, there is no corresponding word for *arĕte*. The closest word or phrase is *tehillah*, for "praise" or "praise-worthy deeds" as found in Isaiah 42:8, 12; 43:21 and 63:7. Putting this together with the above definition, one implication is that this quality is part of, and comes from, a relationship with the one truly worthy of our praise. "The nearness of God is my good" (Psalm 73:28).

A description of Esther's situation and opportunity illustrates this character quality in her life. When her uncle, Mordecai, came to her to counsel her on the Jews' terrible plight under the King, this is what he said. (Remember, she was one of the king's wives.)

> Then Mordecai told them to reply to Esther, "Do not imagine that you in the king's palace can escape any more than all the Jews. For if you remain silent at this time, relief and deliverance will arise for the Jews from another place and you and your father's house will perish. *And who knows whether you have not attained royalty for such a time as this?*" (Esther 4:13–14)

1. Robertson, *Word Pictures*, 151.

The Next Step

This last phrase ties this story into the definition of arĕte. Part of the idea of the word comes from a person or thing accomplishing well that for which it was created. Esther shows us how we can apply this quality to our lives. As we respond to situations — in God-honoring ways, not wavering — we are exhibiting moral excellence (arĕte) in our lives.

Paul especially challenges me to grow in moral strength and conviction in Ephesians 5:11 and 12, where he writes, "Do not participate in the unfruitful deeds of darkness, but instead even expose them; for it is disgraceful even to speak of the things which are done by them in secret." I grow in moral excellence as I honor God with my choices when others see me and when they don't. I grow in this quality as I look to God for strength in each of my decisions and do the right thing in His eyes.

Another very practical thing we can do is to make the same commitment Job made in Job 31:1: "I made a covenant with my eyes not to look with lust upon a young woman" (New Living Translation).

As Peter addresses the quality of moral excellence we are to add to our faith, he probably thought back to when he lacked moral strength to testify for the Lord before His crucifixion. Christ in His grace forgave Peter and restored him. We see later in the book of Acts that Peter did grow in moral strength and courage (see Acts 12).

What about grace?

I've included a quote from the *Dictionary of NT Theology* to show how God's grace is involved here:

> It must be said that the Stoic's view of himself as autonomous in his virtues, is one completely foreign to the NT. Here the virtues are the fruit of the Spirit (Gal. 5:22), subservient to mutual love and the glorification of God. Hence, the NT virtues are not derived from the harmony of the soul (Plato) nor from the quality of the man (Aristotle), but are seen as gracious gifts (charisma) of the divine Spirit: they are the acts and the marks of God's new creation.[2]

As this quote illustrates, the quality of moral excellence is a gracious gift from God.

In the "Lord's Prayer" (Matthew 6:13), Christ includes this phrase: "And do not lead us into temptation, but deliver us from evil." This tells me that my

---

2. Brown, *New Testament Theology*, 927.

Moral Excellence

ability to make a good moral decision in resisting sin comes from God. I ask for His help in this because He is gracious, not because I deserve it.

Ministry Skills: "8 to 15"

In *8 to 15*, Tom Mercer introduces us to the concept of *oikos*. *Oikos* is the Greek word found in the New Testament for "household" or "extended household." An example of where it is used can be found in Acts 16:31: "They said, 'Believe in the Lord Jesus, and you will be saved, you and your household.'" Tom goes on to show how we can apply that today:

> Oikos (or "8 to 15") is the strategy Jesus chose to build His church. It is reflected in everything Jesus did, taught and lived. The oikos model gives every believer the opportunity to be God's instrument in the most effective arena possible, their own circle of relationships. Here's how it works. God has given each of us, on average, anywhere from eight to fifteen people whom He has supernaturally and strategically placed in our relational worlds. The Greeks used one word to describe this personal world—oikos, or "extended household." This is the world He wants to use each of us to change, our individual world![3]

Continue to use the "8 to 15" list provided in the first two chapters. As you develop the daily habit of beginning your day with the Lord, use it every morning as you do so, praying for those God has brought into your life. Remember these guidelines: "Pray that they would each sense God's presence in their lives and that God would draw each one to Himself. Offer yourself every day as an instrument in that process. Watch for appropriate opportunities to discuss and demonstrate your faith with them, as well as invite them to church."[4]

> To the Disciple: Remember: *God wants to change the world.* He wants people you rub shoulders with every day to trust Him as their savior. "For God so loved the world that He gave His only begotten Son, that *whoever* believes in Him shall not perish, but have eternal life." Praying for those on your list is in line with God's heart.

---

3. Mercer, *8 to 15*, 34.
4. Mercer, directions on the "8 to 15" prayer card.

The Next Step

> To the Discipler: Take some time each week to pray together. We can tell someone they need to pray, but we teach them to pray by praying with them. Remember, more is caught than taught.

Personal Worship

Are you taking the time to reflect on the worship and praise songs at the end of each chapter? This may be new to you, but I would encourage you to keep trying it throughout the whole book. Growing up on a farm, there were times when I was working on my own that I sang through the choruses that I'd sing each week in church or youth group. The ideal time was when I was driving a noisy tractor, not worried in the least about others hearing me. Those were great times to worship the Lord and focus on His goodness to me. One reason I have included this part of the weekly study was to return to that time of personally worshipping and praising the Lord. So, worship away!

For growing in moral excellence, I've included "Everlasting God" because it reminds me where I get my strength to be morally strong and courageous. I've also included "Amazing Grace" because it tells of how God has changed us.

"Everlasting God"

Strength will rise as we wait upon the Lord
We will wait upon the Lord
We will wait upon the Lord

Our God, You reign forever
Our hope, our Strong Deliverer
You are the everlasting God
The everlasting God
You do not faint
You won't grow weary

Our God, You reign forever
Our hope, our Strong Deliverer
You are the everlasting God
The everlasting God
You do not faint
You won't grow weary

> You're the defender of the weak
> You comfort those in need
> You lift us up on wings like eagles[5]

"Amazing Grace"

> Amazing Grace, how sweet the sound,
> That saved a wretch like me.
> I once was lost but now am found,
> Was blind, but now I see.
>
> T'was Grace that taught my heart to fear.
> And Grace, my fears relieved.
> How precious did that Grace appear
> The hour I first believed.
>
> Through many dangers, toils and snares
> I have already come;
> 'Tis Grace that brought me safe thus far
> and Grace will lead me home.
>
> The Lord has promised good to me.
> His word my hope secures.
> He will my shield and portion be,
> As long as life endures.
>
> Yea, when this flesh and heart shall fail,
> And mortal life shall cease,
> I shall possess within the veil,
> A life of joy and peace.
>
> When we've been there ten thousand years
> Bright shining as the sun.
> We've no less days to sing God's praise
> Than when we've first begun.[6]

Consider This: (For Group Discussion)

1. Review the verse study for Joshua 1:9.

5. Brenton Gifford Brown, Kenneth Henry Riley (EMI Christian Music Publishing, 2005).
6. John Newton, Public Domain.

The Next Step

2. How does Joshua 1:9 relate to the topic of this chapter, Moral Excellence?

3. What are some of the life decisions facing you now?

4. How would having moral excellence or moral courage affect those decisions?

5. What areas of temptation are you wrestling with, that you need God's strength to overcome?

6. Any thoughts on meditating on the worship songs at the end of each chapter?

Chapter 4

God as Morally Excellent

As you can see from the content page, after looking at a character quality we are to grow in one week, the next week we look at an attribute of God that corresponds to that character quality. In studying moral excellence, there are actually more usages of the word for moral excellence, *arĕte*, referring to God than to us. So this week we will look at what it means that God is morally excellent.

Start your time with the Lord in prayer. You can refer to the examples I gave you on page 13. Another prayer that Paul prays for the believers at Philippi is in Philippians 1:9–11:

> And this I pray, that your love may abound still more and more in real knowledge and all discernment, so that you may approve the things that are excellent, in order to be sincere and blameless until the day of Christ; having been filled with the fruit of righteousness which comes through Jesus Christ, to the glory and praise of God.

> To the Disciple: When faced with a difficult situation or an unsolved dilemma, remember to pray, asking God for an answer or idea. We have the privilege to pray, so spend much time in prayer.

Now, read Isaiah 63:7: "I will make mention of the lovingkindnesses of the Lord, the *praises* of the Lord, according to all that the Lord has granted us, and the great goodness toward the house of Israel, which He has granted

The Next Step

them according to His compassion and according to the abundance of His lovingkindnesses."

- How have you experienced God's lovingkindnesses?

- What has God granted you?

- How has God been good to you?

- How have you experienced God's compassion?

Next, copy 1 Peter 2:9 onto a 3-by-5 card and read it several times. Keep it with your other cards and review them now. Keep working on memorizing these verses and review them daily. Keep handing the Holy Spirit these tools to use in your life.

> To the Discipler: More can be accomplished one-on-one or man-to-man than in a larger group. Take the time to get together individually with those you meet and personalize your time to that person's need.

God as Morally Excellent

Journaling

If you're journaling through the workbook, go to the Journaling section and write down something God has taught you in this lesson so far and respond to God with a prayer.

Verse Study

As you work on memorizing 1 Peter 2:9, begin asking yourself some of the questions from the verse study. They will help you meditate or contemplate these verses throughout the week.

Verse: 1 Peter 2:9

Context:

Who is speaking? Who is the audience? What is the subject? What is the time frame, beginning and ending thought?

Key Words:

In light of the definitions, how do they expand or highlight this verse for me?

The Next Step

Cross References:

Verses that support my understanding of this verse.

For Discussion:

- What is the main issue being addressed here?

- What about this verse is challenging for me to believe?

- What sinful thinking or behavior does this verse expose in me?

- What would applying this truth in my life look like?

- How can we encourage one another in the truth of this verse?

God as Morally Excellent

In this chapter we are looking at God as Morally Excellent. It will be important to recognize that moral excellence as applied to God has a different definition than when applied to man. Applied to man, moral excellence is defined as strength of character with moral implications. It involves both moral strength and the will to act. Applied to God, moral excellence describes the perfection of all of God's attributes, not just those we associated with morality. This will help as you look at this attribute applied to God.

As mentioned in the last chapter, there is no corresponding word for *arĕte* in the Old Testament. The closest word or phrase is *tehillah*, which means "praise" or "praiseworthy deeds."

Another Hebrew word similar to the Greek arĕte is *hode*. In two occurrences, the Hebrew word *hode* is used, translated into English as "majesty" or "glory." In Habakkuk 3:3 we read, "God comes from Teman, and the Holy One from Mount Paran. His splendor covers the heavens, and the earth is full of His *praise*."

In *Strong's*, *hode* is defined as grandeur, beauty, comeliness, glorious, glory, honour or majesty and is being descriptive of God. The other place is Zechariah, referring to Joshua.[1]

In 1 Peter 2:9 and 2 Peter 1:3, God's arĕte is mentioned speaking of His perfection or excellence. God's praiseworthy acts are to be proclaimed by His people and His attribute of perfection is to be recognized by all men.

Peter writes in 1 Peter 2:9, "But you are a chosen race, a royal priesthood, a holy nation, a people for God's own possession, so that you may proclaim the *excellencies* of Him who called you out of darkness into His marvelous light."

This is God's attribute of perfection. God is morally excellent as He is perfect in all of His attributes. One product of God acting on all His attributes is to accomplish our salvation. He is the one who is worthy to be God and called God — the only One. "Because of what we are it is our great function that by word and by deed, by our confession and by our conduct we at all times and under all circumstances publish in our own midst and to all men about us him who called us out of darkness, etc. True believers cannot keep still; they simply must speak out with lip and with life. Thus they function as a royal priesthood and ever offer up sacrifices of praise and thanksgiving."[2]

---

1. Strong, *Strong's Exhaustive Concordance*, page 123 in the "A Concise Dictionary of the words in the Hebrew Bible."

2. Lenski, *Interpretation of I and II Epistles of Peter*, 103.

The Next Step

In Peter's second letter to scattered believers, he writes in chapter 1, verse 3, "Seeing that His divine power has granted to us everything pertaining to life and godliness, through the true knowledge of Him who called us by His own glory and *excellence*." God's reaching out and choosing and saving us is according to this quality of excellence.

> God has called believers 'by his own glory (*doxa*) and goodness (arĕte), that is, God in salvation reveals his splendor and his moral excellence, and these are means he uses to effect conversions.[3]

God's working out a plan whereby He purchases our salvation is a declaration to the world of His excellence. A wonderful part of the character of God is to have compassion for people and save them. This is part of God being God, of God being morally excellent.

We see this come together in Isaiah 61:1, 10 and 11:

> The spirit of the Lord God is upon me, because the Lord has anointed me to bring good news to the afflicted; He has sent me to bind up the brokenhearted, to proclaim liberty to captives and freedom to prisoners; I will rejoice greatly in the Lord, my soul will exult in my God; for He has clothed me with garments of salvation, He has wrapped me with a robe of righteousness, as a bridegroom decks himself with a garland, and as a bride adorns herself with her jewels. For as the earth brings forth its sprouts, and as a garden causes the things sown in it to spring up, so the Lord God will cause righteousness and *praise* to spring up before all the nations.

Our salvation is a declaration to the world around us of God's excellence. What a wonderful thought. Along this line, an implication to this is that if God being morally excellent means the perfection of all His attributes, then the working out of our salvation is a proclamation to the world of the perfection of God's every attribute. Every attribute was involved in the plan of salvation through the death and burial and resurrection of Christ. You can look at each attribute and see how they're used and satisfied in Christ's work of salvation for mankind.

We must visit one more area of the Bible. The "praiseworthiness" aspect of all this leads me to look at Revelation 4: 11 and 5:9 and 12 and to look at the word "worthy." In these verses, we see the elders worshipping Christ with these songs of His worthiness:

---

3. Gaebelein, *The Expositor's Bible Commentary*, 267.

"Worthy are You, our Lord and our God, to receive glory and honor and power; for You created all things, and because of Your will they existed, and were created."

"Worthy are You to take the book and to break its seals; for You were slain, and purchased for God with Your blood men from every tribe and tongue and people and nation. You have made them to be a kingdom and priests to our God; and they will reign upon the earth."

"Worthy is the Lamb that was slain to receive power and riches and wisdom and might and honor and glory and blessing."

Again, it is interesting to note that Christ's worthiness and accomplishing our salvation are tied together in these passages.

What about grace?

I will just repeat one phrase from above to highlight how God's grace is all over this quality of His Moral Excellence. *Our salvation is a declaration to the world around us of God's excellence.* And our salvation is only by God's grace!

Ministry Skills: "8 to 15"

"When the truth that God put us here for a reason — to be a part of the greatest initiative in the history of mankind — burrows deep roots into a believer's soul, and they understand that no one else can fulfill that purpose in their relational world as well as they can, then something transformational happens."[4]

Take a minute and reflect on the significance of that statement. When you begin to look over those you have listed on your card, you begin to realize God has given you a unique opportunity to pray for them. As we engage in their lives, we realize what an amazing purpose and opportunity we have.

Next week we will talk more about "engaging" with those God has supernaturally placed in your life, but for now continue to pray for them and ask God to draw them to Himself.

---

4. Mercer, *8 to 15*, 46.

The Next Step

> To the Disciple: "Prayer is God speaking into existence through human lips," Dawson Trotman, writing in his journal about the value of being in the Bible and praying (Betty Lee Skinner, *Daws*).

Personal Worship

Keep up your times of personal worship. Carry these songs as you go about your day.

"So God now is seeking worshipers who will bring Him glory, not just for an hour on Sunday, but every day through all their activities. We can't properly worship God on Sundays if we're not worshiping Him throughout the week."[5]

For thinking about God as Morally Excellent, I've included "Come and See" and "God of Wonders."

"Come and See"

Come and see the glory of the Lord, come behold the Lamb.
Come and know the mercy of the King, bowing down before Him

For He is Lord above the heavens, Lord in all the earth,
Lord of all creations, Worthy to be served
Hal—le—lu—jah. Hal—le—lu—jah.

Come and give thanks unto the Lord, come behold the Lamb.
Come and sing the praises of the King, bowing down before Him.[6]

"God of Wonders"

Lord of all creation of water earth and sky
The heavens are your Tabernacle
Glory to the Lord on high
[Chorus:]
God of wonders beyond our galaxy You are Holy, Holy
The universe declares your Majesty And you are holy holy
Lord of Heaven and Earth, Lord of Heaven and Earth

---

5. Cole, "True Worship."
6. Author Unknown, Public Domain.

Early in the morning I will celebrate the light
When I stumble in the darkness I will call your name by night
[Chorus]
Lord of heaven and earth, lord of heaven and earth
Hallelujah to the lord of heaven and earth [repeat 3 times]
Holy . . . holy . . . holy god . . .
[Chorus]
Precious lord reveal your heart to me . . .
Father holy . . .
[background] . . . Lord god almighty . . .
The universe declares your majesty
You are holy, holy, holy, holy,
Hallelujah to the lord of heaven and earth [6x][7]

Consider This: (For Group Discussion)

1. Review the key points of the verse study for 1 Peter 2:9.

2. How would giving a clear testimony of your salvation contribute to knowing and proclaiming God being morally excellent?

3. Pick an attribute of God and write down how it is used in God accomplishing our salvation.

4. What is something new you have learned about God through this study (or something old re-enforced)?

7. Chris Tomlin (Brentwood Benson Music).

The Next Step

5. What helps you (or could help you) remember to pray for those on your "8 to 15" list?

6. What was the most helpful part of this study for you this week?

CHAPTER 5

Knowledge

Now we add the character quality of Knowledge to moral excellence: "Now for this very reason also, applying all diligence, in your faith supply moral excellence, and in your moral excellence, knowledge" (2 Peter 1:5). The word Peter uses is *gnosin*. *Vines Dictionary* notes that this word is primarily "a seeking to know, an inquiry, investigation," especially of spiritual truth.[1] Usually when we think of knowledge, we think about a set amount of content or information. As we look at the character quality of knowledge we will lean more toward a desire to know, especially as it related to our knowing God and His revelation in the Bible.

Start your time with the Lord in prayer. Consider Philippians 3:10 and 11 as a prayer as you begin this chapter:

- "That I may know Him and the power of His resurrection and the fellowship of His sufferings, being conformed to His death; in order that I may attain to the resurrection from the dead."

- When I come to this section of Paul's letter to the Philippians I pray for this same hunger to know the Lord.

---

1. Vine et al., *Vine's Complete Expository Dictionary*, 348.

The Next Step

> To the Disciple: Asking for help is a very important and legitimate part of prayer. In the same way that my kids honor me as their dad when they ask my help or advice, we honor God as our Father when we ask Him for wisdom or help.

Now, read Psalm 27:4–6: *"One thing I have asked from the Lord, that I shall seek: That I may dwell in the house of the Lord all the days of my life, to behold the beauty of the Lord and to meditate in His temple. For in the day of trouble He will conceal me in His tabernacle; in the secret place of His tent He will hide me; He will lift me up on a rock. And now my head will be lifted up above my enemies around me, and I will offer in His tent sacrifices with shouts of joy; I will sing, yes, I will sing praises to the Lord."*

- What is David asking for in these verses?

- What would you ask of God along this line?

Next, copy Philippians 3:8 onto a 3-by-5 card as your next verse to memorize and study in the verse-study section. Keep it with your other cards and review them now. Keep working on memorizing these verses and review them daily. Keep handing the Holy Spirit these tools to use in your life.

> To the Discipler: Try to set some time aside daily to pray for those with whom you meet. Look for ways to reinforce and remind you to pray for them, such as at each meal or during a regular coffee break.

Journaling

Go to the journaling section and write something God has taught you in this lesson so far and respond to God with a prayer.

Verse Study

As you work on memorizing Philippians 3:8, ask yourself some of the questions from the verse study. For instance, what does Paul mean by gaining Christ? They will help you meditate or chew on these verses throughout the week.

Verse: Philippians 3:8

Context:

Who is speaking? Who is the audience? What is the subject? What is the time frame, beginning and ending thought?

Key Words:

In light of the definitions, how do they expand or highlight this verse for me?

The Next Step

Cross References:

Verses that support my understanding of this verse.

For Discussion:

- What is the main issue being addressed here?

- What about this verse is challenging for me to believe?

- What sinful thinking or behavior does this verse expose in me?

- What would applying this truth in my life look like?

- How can we encourage one another in the truth of this verse?

Knowledge

In this chapter we are looking at growing in *knowledge* as a character quality. As mentioned earlier, the word Peter uses for knowledge is *gnosin*, which means a seeking to know, or an inquiry or investigation, especially of spiritual truth.

In *Brown's Dictionary of New Testament Theology*, the author writes, "the noun gnosis also originally expressed the act of knowing through experience."[2] The idea here is practical wisdom, "the wisdom which distinguishes the good from the bad, and shows the way of flight from the bad."[3] "This knowledge is gained in the practical exercise of goodness, which in turn, leads to a fuller knowledge of Christ."[4]

Paul, in Philippians 1:9–11, illustrates this kind of knowledge:

> And this I pray, that your love may abound still more and more in real knowledge and all discernment, so that you may approve the things that are excellent, in order to be sincere and blameless until the day of Christ; having been filled with the fruit of righteousness which comes through Jesus Christ, to the glory and praise of God.

These verses in Philippians show how this knowledge has to do with applying God's wisdom to our everyday lives so that we make the best decisions. Praying the above prayer for someone implies that we are praying for someone to grow in love for others through knowledge gained from God. By involving love, we are praying for the best results for the good of others. Knowledge here is very much related to one's everyday life and choices.

Philippians 3:8 illustrates how knowledge is a character quality in that Paul is expressing his strong desire to personally know God and have a close, growing relationship with Him.

Another verse that brings out this sense of knowing God is John 17:3: "This is eternal life, that they may know You, the only true God, and Jesus Christ whom You have sent." It's as if John were saying, "This is really living, to Know God and Jesus Christ whom He sent!"

In the Old Testament, "knowledge of God is always linked with God's acts of self-revelation. This is illustrated in the formula, 'And you shall know that I am Yahweh.'"[5] If knowledge is predicated on the one being known desiring to be known, then our growing in this kind of knowledge implies a desire on our part to know God. As Colin Brown goes on to explain, "we

2. Brown, *New Testament Theology*, 392.
3. Green, *New Testament Commentaries*, 68.
4. Ibid.
5. Brown, *New Testament Theology*, 395.

can know God only as we know Jesus Christ (Phil. 3:10; cf. Col. 2:2f). But Christ is not to be known through theological speculation, but rather as one is met by him and as one acknowledges him as the Lord (Phil. 3:8)."[6] Content comes into play as we read and study the Bible. When we learn more about God in a relationship, we want to get to know Him even more.

To sum up: With this virtue, Peter is not talking about a set amount of information alone, but the character quality of being an eager learner and someone who has grown in Godly knowledge and is able to apply that "knowledge" or wisdom to everyday life. I grow in the quality of knowledge as I ask God for a hunger to know Him and as I spend time with God in His Word. "O taste and see that the Lord is good" (Psalm 34:8).

What about grace?

When I think of our ability and privilege to personally know God and have a relationship with Him, I am reminded of Psalm 8:

> O Lord, our Lord, how majestic is Your name in all the earth, who have displayed Your splendor above the heavens. From the mouth of infants and nursing babes You have established strength because of Your adversaries, to make the enemy and the revengeful cease. When I consider Your heavens, the work of Your fingers, the moon and the stars, which You have ordained; what is man that You take thought of him, and the son of man that You care for him? Yet You have made him a little lower than God, and You crown him with glory and majesty."

It is by God's grace that we can know God and that He, a holy God, would make a way for us to have His Son's righteousness, that we might live with Him forever. This is all by His grace.

Ministry Skills: "8 to 15"

As you have been praying for your *oikos*, or extended household, have you become curious about the people on your list? I have found that as I've prayed for those God has put in my life, I have wondered about their church background or family upbringing. I have wondered if they've heard the gospel and understood it. I have wondered if they've ever asked God for

---

6. Ibid. 402.

help in a difficult situation. I have learned that God is working in people's lives in ways I never knew. In fact, God is often drawing people to Himself that I would have concluded had no interest in God.

When it comes to engaging with those for whom I'm praying, I begin by asking questions to get to know them. Ask questions that address the thoughts and questions just mentioned. Be sure to ask them questions to really get to know them, not to turn the conversation right to the gospel and their need to pray a prayer right now. Get to know them. Show them you really care about them. God is working on their hearts and He will open doors as you get to know them and make yourself available in genuine love.

> To the Disciple: Preparing hearts for the gospel begins with asking questions before answering questions that haven't yet been asked.

> To the Discipler: We can model genuine interest in others by showing genuine interest in those with whom we meet. Be sure to ask questions. We all tend to talk more about ourselves than ask questions and listen.

Personal Worship

In Pastor Cole's message on "The Priority of True Worship," he points out how as believers we are sometimes man-centered.[7] We worship in this way if there is too much attention to performance or if the words we are singing are more focused on our selves and not on the God we are worshiping. This is where scriptural songs are especially helpful.

Keep up your times of personal worship. Carry these songs with you as you go about your day. For thinking about growing in Knowledge, I've included these two:

"Sweet Hour of Prayer"

> 1. Sweet hour of prayer! sweet hour of prayer!
> That calls me from a world of care,
> And bids me at my Father's throne

---

7. Cole, "True Worship," 3.

The Next Step

Make all my wants and wishes known.
In seasons of distress and grief,
My soul has often found relief,
And oft escaped the tempter's snare,
By thy return, sweet hour of prayer!

2. Sweet hour of prayer! sweet hour of prayer!
The joys I feel, the bliss I share,
Of those whose anxious spirits burn
With strong desires for thy return!
With such I hasten to the place
Where God my Savior shows His face,
And gladly take my station there,
And wait for thee, sweet hour of prayer!

3. Sweet hour of prayer! sweet hour of prayer!
Thy wings shall my petition bear
To Him whose truth and faithfulness
Engage the waiting soul to bless.
And since He bids me seek His face,
Believe His Word and trust His grace,
I'll cast on Him my every care,
And wait for thee, sweet hour of prayer!

Sweet hour of prayer! sweet hour of prayer!
May I thy consolation share,
Till, from Mount Pisgah's lofty height,
I view my home and take my flight.
This robe of flesh I'll drop, and rise
To seize the everlasting prize,
And shout, while passing through the air,
"Farewell, farewell, sweet hour of prayer!".[8]

"I Will Offer Up My Life"

I will offer up my life In spirit and truth
Pouring out the oil of love As my worship to You
In surrender I must give my every part
Lord, receive the sacrifice Of a broken heart

CHORUS:
Jesus, what can I give, what can I bring

---

8. William W. Walford, Public Domain.

Knowledge

> To so faithful a friend, to so loving a King
> Savior, what can be said, what can be sung
> As a praise of Your name
> For the things You have done
> Oh my words could not tell, not even in part
> Of the debt of love that is owed By this thankful heart
>
> You deserve my every breath For You've paid the great cost
> Giving up Your life to death Even death on a cross
> You took all my shame away There defeated my sin
> Opened up the gates of heaven And have beckoned me in[9]

Consider This: (For Group Discussion)

1. Review and be ready to share what you learned from the verse study on Philippians 3:8.

2. So, how can knowledge be a character quality?

3. What are some practical ways you could work on this quality this month?

4. What are some things you have wondered about with those on your "8 to 15" list?

---

9. Matt Redman (EMI Christian Music Publishing).

The Next Step

5. How has looking at grace each week helped in this study?

6. Periodically I hear someone speak negatively about "head knowledge." How can head knowledge be bad, and what is the remedy?

CHAPTER 6

God as All-Knowing

The attribute of God corresponding to our growing in Knowledge is that of God being All-Knowing, or His Omniscience. In John 3:20, John says that God knows all things. In this chapter we will explore what that means and how it impacts our lives.

Start your time with the Lord in prayer: Psalm 139:23 and 24 would be an appropriate prayer for this chapter, as it is David's prayer after his meditation on how completely God knew him: *"Search me, O God, and know my heart; try me and know my anxious thoughts; and see if there be any hurtful way in me, and lead me in the everlasting way."*

> To the Disciple: How do I come to the Word of God?
> - With humility. (James 1:21)
> - With expectation to see. (Ephesians 1:17–19)
> - With intention to put into practice. (Psalm 119:32)

Now, read Psalm 139:1–6:

> O Lord, You have searched me and known me. You know when I sit down and when I rise up; You understand my thought from afar. You scrutinize my path and my lying down, and are intimately acquainted with all my ways. Even before there is a word on my tongue, behold, O Lord, You know it all. You have enclosed me

The Next Step

behind and before, and laid Your hand upon me. Such knowledge is too wonderful for me; it is too high, I cannot attain to it."

How does this passage personalize the idea of God knowing all things?

Next, copy I Samuel 16:7 onto a 3-by-5 card as your next verse to memorize and study in the verse study section. If memorizing comes hard to you, you might memorize the second half of this verse, but still look at the whole verse in the following verse study. "For God sees not as man sees, for man looks at the outward appearance, but the Lord looks at the heart." Keep it with your other cards and review them now. Keep working on memorizing these verses and review them daily. Keep handing the Holy Spirit these tools to use in your life.

> To the Discipler: As you work on memorizing these verses, let them guide you in praying for those you're discipling. You will be participating with the Holy Spirit as God works these verses into their lives.

Journaling

Writing can be a wonderful ministry in the lives of others. As you write down what God has taught you, you might think of someone who'd be encouraged by what you've learned. Write them a note of encouragement that includes a verse and how God spoke to you through that verse.

Verse Study

As you work on memorizing I Samuel 16:7, ask yourself some of the questions from the verse study. For instance, what does God see when He looks at my heart and what does that even mean? They will help you meditate upon or contemplate these verses throughout the week.

God as All-Knowing

Verse: I Samuel 16:7

Context:

Who is speaking? Who is the audience? What is the subject? What is the time frame, beginning and ending thought?

Key Words:

In light of the definitions, how do they expand or highlight this verse for me?

Cross References:

(Verses that support my understanding of this verse.

For Discussion:

- What is the main issue being addressed here?

The Next Step

- What about this verse is challenging for me to believe?

- What sinful thinking or behavior does this verse expose in me?

- What would applying this truth in my life look like?

- How can we encourage one another in the truth of this verse?[1]

God's omniscience, or all-knowing nature, can be defined in this way: "God fully knows Himself and all things actual and possible in one simple and eternal act."[2] Dr. Wayne Grudem expands much more on this definition in addressing God's holiness and knowledge. In 1 John 1:5 we read, "God is light and in Him is no darkness at all." "In this context 'light' has a suggestion of both moral purity and full knowledge or awareness. If there is 'no darkness at all' in God, but He is entirely 'light,' then God is Himself both entirely holy and also entirely filled with self-knowledge."[3]

Keeping all this in mind, let me give you three personal implications about God's knowledge as it relates to us:

1. From Psalm 139: God knew everything about me when He made me and He is also accomplishing all of His plans and purposes. Therefore, He made me and designed me to be a part of those plans. Paul

---

1. Sloan, "Forums of Four" (2000).
2. Grudem, *Systematic Theology*, 190.
3. Ibid. 190.

continues with this idea in Ephesians 2:10: "For we are *His workmanship*, created in Christ Jesus *for good works*, which God prepared beforehand so that we would walk in them."

If God knows me inside and out and is working in me to make me His workmanship, I can look for what God is doing in me and work with Him in seeing that develop in my life. That is what Paul is saying in Philippians 2:12 and 13: "Work out your salvation with fear and trembling; for it is God who is at work in you, both to will and to work for His good pleasure."

2. God knows us completely and "spoke" the scriptures we have in the Bible for our good. Paul reminds us of the value of God's word in our lives in 2 Timothy 2:16 and 17: "All scripture is inspired by God and profitable for teaching, for reproof, for correction, for training in righteousness; so that the man of God may be adequate, equipped for every good work." Therefore, His word is designed to help us walk with Him and is an amazing help for us. Put another way, scripture can show us how to walk with the Lord. It can show us when and how we stop walking with Him, how to get back to walking with the Lord and how to keep from straying.

3. Included in His knowledge is His understanding of us, and the author of Hebrews implies that because of this, we should therefore "draw near to Him," or as we might say today, "Run to Him now and often!"

> Therefore, since we have a great high priest who has passed through the heavens Jesus the Son of God, let us hold fast our confession. For we do not have a high priest who cannot sympathize with our weaknesses, but One who has been tempted in all things as we are, yet without sin. Therefore let us draw near with confidence to the throne of grace, so that we may receive mercy and find grace to help in time of need. (Hebrews 4:14–16)

We have someone who knows us this well and has all resources at His command. In fact, He made all the resources. He cares about us enough to think about us all the time (Psalm 139). Shouldn't we want to draw close to Him?

> To the Disciple: We grow as believers as we spend time with the Lord in His word and in prayer, working out in our lives what He is working on in us. This way God is directing and accomplishing our growth.

The Next Step

What about grace?

One of the verses we looked at was Ephesians 2:10 and how we are God's workmanship. Leading up to this, in verse 8, Paul tells us that we are saved by grace, as a gift, and that this is not of ourselves or because we deserve it. Verse 10 continues this idea of God working in us by grace when he describes us as God's workmanship. He is the reason we can know Him and become usable for Him.

In Hebrews 4:14 to 16, we saw how we can draw near to God because He not only knows us but also understands us. In verse 13 of that chapter, the author tells us that "there is no creature hidden from His sight, but all things are open and laid bare to the eyes of Him with whom we have to do."

When I think about being married for 34 years, the amazing thing to me is that after all this time and my wife knowing me as well as she does, she still loves me, maybe more than ever. I'm a great procrastinator. I'm not always patient, nor always a good listener. In fact, I could fill a book with the things I do wrong that my wife has clearly seen. But, she still loves me. That's grace on her part.

The place of grace and the knowledge of God is that God knows me completely. This includes all that I will do and say and think. He still loves me and I am His workmanship.

Ministry Skills: "8 to 15"

As you pray for those on your "8 to 15" list this week, are you getting to know them? Is there a context where they would enjoy getting together and "catching up"? Brainstorm for a few minutes and list all the ways you could meet with the people on your list and get to know them better.

1.

2.

3.

4.

5.

6.

7.

God as All-Knowing

I asked you to think of a context they would enjoy because we are going into their world, not asking them to fit into ours. Part of the idea of the Incarnational ministry of Christ was that He left His home in heaven and became a man and lived in our world. What can we do to *go* to those we care about, not wait for them to come to us?

> To the Disciple: It really is true: People don't care what we know until they know that we care.

> To the Discipler: We can model an Incarnational ministry by bringing those we are discipling with us as we visit our 8 to 15.

Personal Worship

"But an hour is coming, and now is, when the true worshipers will worship the Father in spirit and truth; for such people the Father seeks to be His worshipers. God is spirit, and those who worship Him must worship in spirit and truth" (John 4:23–24).

> To be true worshipers, we must worship both in spirit and in truth. To worship in spirit without truth is to worship false gods. To worship in truth without spirit is to fall into dead orthodoxy. We may be doctrinally correct, but we're lifeless. And, the Father must be the focus of our worship."[4]

Keep up your times of personal worship. Carry these songs with you as you go about your day. For thinking about God as All-Knowing, I've included these two songs:

"Before There Was Time"

Before there was time,
There were visions in Your mind.
There was death in the fall of mankind,
But there was life in salvation's design.
Before there were days,
There were nights I could not see Your face,
But the night couldn't keep me from grace

---

4. Cole, "True Worship."

The Next Step

When You came and took my place.
So I cry, "Holy, only begotten Son of God,
Ancient of Days."
I cry, "Holy, only begotten Son of God."
And sing the praises
Of the One who saved me, And the promises He made.

Before there was time,
You counted the hairs on my head.
You knew all the words that I've said,
And You purchased me back from the dead.
And before I was made,
You searched me and knew my ways.
You numbered all of my days
And You set forth the steps I would take.

So I cry, "Holy, only begotten Son of God,
Ancient of Days."
I cry, "Holy, only begotten Son of God."
And sing the praises
Of the One who saved me, And the promises He made.

Well, You saved me. And You raised me.
You saved me.
And You pulled me from the grave.

So I cry, "Holy, only begotten Son of God,
Ancient of Days."
I cry, "Holy, only begotten Son of God."
And sing the praises
I cry, "Holy, only begotten Son of God,
Ancient of Days."
I cry, "Holy, only begotten Son of God."
And sing the praises
Of the One who saved me,
And the promises He made
Before there was time.[5]

---

5 Aaron Senseman (Music Services, 2001).

"He Knows My Name"

I have a Maker
He formed my heart
Before even time began
My life was in his hands

I have a Father
He calls me His own
He'll never leave me
No matter where I go

He knows my name
He knows my every thought
He sees each tear that falls
And He hears me when I call[6]

Consider This: (For Group Discussion)

1. What has happened in your life that God has used to demonstrate His knowledge of all things, and especially all things related to you?

2. Review the study of I Samuel 16:7, highlighting what you've learned.

3. When the author of Hebrews tells us to draw near to God, how do you understand this?

---

6. Tommy Walker (Universal Music—Brentwood Benson Songs, 1996).

The Next Step

4. What are some ways that you draw near to God? What new ways can you draw near to Him?

5. How do you understand the place of grace in God knowing you completely?

6. What is a highlight of this chapter for you this week?

CHAPTER 7

Self-Control

The character quality we are to add to *Knowledge* is *Self-Control*. The Greek word Peter uses is *egkrateia*. The word means "self-control," "mastery," or self-denial, "not only in food and drink, but in every aspect of life."[1] Self-control really comes down to living a spirit-controlled life. Apart from the Holy Spirit, we do not have control or the ability to resist sin. In this chapter we will study how to grow in self-control as God strengthens us through the Holy Spirit.

Start your time with the Lord in prayer, asking God to guard your heart and mind. Philippians 4:6 and 7 address this:

> Be anxious for nothing, but in everything by prayer and supplication with thanksgiving let your requests be made known to God. And the peace of God, which surpasses all comprehension, will guard your hearts and your minds in Christ Jesus.

> To the Disciple: Look for different ways to spend time with the Lord in prayer. Sometimes I find it helps to take a walk and pour my heart out to God. David seems to be saying this in Psalm 62, verse 8: "Trust in Him at all times, O people; Pour out your heart before Him; God is a refuge for us."

---

1. Green, *New Testament Commentaries*, 68.

The Next Step

Now, read Psalm 62:5–8: "My soul, wait in silence for God only, for my hope is from Him. He only is my rock and my salvation, my stronghold; I shall not be shaken. On God my salvation and my glory rest; the rock of my strength, my refuge is in God. Trust in Him at all times, O people; pour out your heart before Him; God is a refuge for us."

How is God a rock or a stronghold for you?

Next, copy Galatians 5:16 onto a 3-by-5 card for your next verse to memorize and study in the verse study section. Keep it with your other cards and review them now. Keep working on memorizing these verses and review them daily.

> To the Discipler: Be sure to take the time to review the memory verses each week with those who meet with you. This will reinforce the importance of scripture memory and provide accountability for him/her and ourselves. Be sure to focus more on the meaning of the verses than every word being perfect.

Journaling

Go to the journal section and write something that God has taught you in this lesson so far, and respond to God with a prayer.

Verse Study

Galatians 5:16 does not use the phrase "self-control," but it does address the key for growing in the fruit of the spirit as mentioned in verses 22–23. Be sure to spend a little extra time looking at the context of Gal. 5:16.

Verse: Galatians 5:16

Context:

Who is speaking? Who is the audience? What is the subject? What is the time frame, beginning and ending thought?

Key Words:

In light of the definitions, how do they expand or highlight this verse for me?

Cross References:

Verses that support my understanding of this verse.

For Discussion:

- What is the main issue being addressed here?

The Next Step

- What about this verse is challenging for me to believe?

- What sinful thinking or behavior does this verse expose in me?

- What would applying this truth in my life look like?

- How can we encourage one another in the truth of this verse?

Christian self-control is submission to the control of the indwelling Christ. It especially deals with moral purity. During New Testament times, this word meant controlling the passions instead of being controlled by them. He is not saying to ignore or suppress them, but to keep them under control. As one commentator put it, "Self-control is the exact opposite of the excesses of the false teachers and the sexual abuses in the pagan world."[2]

Self-control is one of the fruits of the spirit listed in Galatians 5:23, and is therefore the fruit of a spirit-filled life. Practically speaking, it is the ability or discipline to apply God's standards to our lives, with the Holy Spirit's help and by God's power. We see it when we deny ourselves and submit to God. We grow in self-control as we grow in the disciplines of our lives.

Four things we can do to help us grow in self-control are: Act like men, Be alert, Be strong in the Lord, and Make a Covenant with your eyes.

2. Gaebelein, *The Expositor's Bible Commentary*, 269.

1. *Act like men*! "Act as free men, and do not use your freedom as a covering for evil, but use it as bondslaves of God" (1 Peter 2:16). One decision we are faced with 24/7 is to use all that God has given us for selfish sinful purposes or to serve the Lord as His bought slave. There is a sense where we have real choices before us and we can look to God for the strength to choose to please and serve Him. Each choice for Him helps us grow stronger in "self-control." Each choice made "as a covering for evil" makes us weaker in "self-control."

2. *Be Alert*! The word for "being alert," used in the New Testament, means to keep awake, to be spiritually alert, to be watchful and vigilant.[3] I can think of no better way to convey the importance of this in our growing in self-control than to list these eight verses:

- "Therefore be on the alert, for you do not know which day your Lord is coming" (Matthew 24:42).
- "Be on the alert then, for you do not know the day nor the hour" (Matthew 25:13).
- "What I say to you I say to all, 'Be on the alert!'" (Mark 13:37)
- "Therefore be on the alert, remembering that night and day for a period of three years I did not cease to admonish each one with tears" (Acts 20:31).
- "Be on the alert, stand firm in the faith, act like men, be strong" (1 Corinthians 16:13).
- "With all prayer and petition pray at all times in the Spirit, and with this in view, be on the alert with all perseverance and petition for all the saints" (Ephesians 6:18).
- "So then let us not sleep as others do, but let us be alert and sober" (1 Thessalonians 5:6).
- "Be of sober spirit, be on the alert. Your adversary, the devil, prowls around like a roaring lion, seeking someone to devour" (1 Peter 5:8).

3. *Be Strong in the Lord*! Reflect back on Joshua 1:9, which you memorized in chapter 3. As you've been reviewing this verse daily, you've been meditating on what it means to be strong in the Lord. One thought that comes to my mind is, "I really need the Lord's strength." Ask Him for it every day as you continue to review and reflect on this

---

3. Vine et al, *Vine's Complete Expository Dictionary*, 667.

verse. Throughout the day, be very specific as you are confronting a particular challenge. Ask for God's strength in facing that situation.

4. *Make a Covenant with your eyes.* In Job 31:1, Job tells us, "I have made a covenant with my eyes; how then could I gaze at a virgin?" This is a promise born out of conviction and great need. Job knew how weak his heart was. He knew he needed the strongest contract or agreement possible with his eyes, the gate to his heart, to not regard a woman in a lustful way.

You and I have to make this covenant in order to grow in self-control. When we fall, we need to quickly return to God for forgiveness and renewal. This is critical because if we do not quickly return to the Lord, it will take our hearts away from the Lord, and it will destroy us (James 1:15).

> To the Disciple: I find that my looking to the Lord for help is not a one-time action but a continual turning to Him. As we do, we are developing the habit of looking to Him, and that includes the strength to do so. (Romans 12:1 speaks of a living sacrifice.)

What about grace?

So where does grace fit into all of this? It is by God's grace that He gives us the strength to resist temptation and "fix our eyes on Christ." It is by God's grace that we are cleansed and renewed in our relationship with Christ when we come back to Him. It is by His grace that we grow in self-control and all the fruits of the spirit.

In 1 Peter 5:8 we were exhorted to be of sober spirit and be on the alert. Two verses later, in verse 10, Peter continues by writing, "After you have suffered for a little while, the *God of all grace*, who called you to His eternal glory in Christ, will Himself perfect, confirm, strengthen and establish you."

Ministry Skills: "8 to 15"

Tom Mercer makes this statement in *8 to 15* about our purpose: "We could also call your oikos your purpose because that group of people actually frames the primary reason for your breathing right now."[4] Later he writes, "We are not in the church simply to make sure we become less and less sinful."[5] Yet hopefully we are becoming less and less sinful, so that we will be a vessel, usable by God (2 Timothy 2:21). What are we trying to be usable for? If God's purpose for the church is to see the lost saved and then grow to the place of sharing that with others, then we ought to be about this. Our purpose individually takes on a very specific focus when we come to realize that God has supernaturally placed a small group of people, usually around 8 to 15, in each of our lives to pray and see God do amazing things for.

Earlier in that same book, Tom challenged my thinking with this statement: "A local church exists, not for herself, but for the sake of the people who don't attend it yet!"[6] By disciplining yourself to daily pray for your "8 to 15," God will turn your heart toward some of those who don't attend yet, but by God's grace will.

I would encourage you to go to 8to15.com and listen to Tom Mercer's heart. He will encourage you as you grow in reaching out to your "8 to 15."

> To the Disciple: When you see God with clarity and believe His Word with immediacy, you will be compelled to act upon it.

> To the Discipler: "Discipline imposed from the outside eventually defeats when it is not matched by desire from within" (*Daws*, page 77). Be sure to encourage those with whom you meet, and pray for them to have a heart to run after God.

Personal Worship

So, how much should our emotions play a part in our worship? "I believe that worship in spirit is, in part, emotional or felt. This is not to say that we should pump up our emotions with music or crowd fervor. Genuine emotions for God stem from focusing our minds on the truth of who He is

---

4. Mercer, *8 to 15*, 54.
5. Ibid.
6. Mercer, *8 to 15*, 14.

The Next Step

and what He has done for us at the cross. But if your worship never touches your emotions, something is wrong." (Steve Cole's "The Priority of True Worship," Aug. 11, 2013)

Keep up your times of personal worship. Have you found it helpful to carry these songs with you as you go about your day? For growing in Self-Control, I've included these two songs:

"Only by Grace"

Only by grace can we enter, Only by grace can we stand
Not by our human endeavor, But by the blood of the Lamb

Into Your presence You call us, You call us to come
Into Your presence You draw us, And now by Your grace we come

Lord, if You mark our transgressions Who would stand
Thanks to Your grace we are cleansed By the blood of the Lamb
Lord, if You mark our transgressions Who would stand
Thanks to Your to Your grace we are cleansed
By the blood of the Lamb[7]

"Come Thou Fount"

Come thou fount of every blessing
Tune my heart to sing thy grace
Streams of mercy never ceasing
Call for songs of loudest praise
Teach me some melodious sonnet
Sung by flaming tongues above.
Praise His Name I'm fixed upon it
Name of God's redeeming love.

Hither to thy love has blessed me
Thou has brought me to this place
And I know thy hand will bring me
Safely home by thy good grace
Jesus sought me when a stranger,
Wandering from the fold of God;
He, to rescue me from danger,
Bought me with His precious blood.

O to grace how great a debtor

---

7. Gerrit Gustafson (Integrity's Hosanna! Music, 1990).

> Daily I'm constrained to be!
> Let Thy goodness, like a fetter,
> Bind my wandering heart to Thee:
> Prone to wander, Lord, I feel it,
> Prone to leave the God I love;
> Here's my heart, O take and seal it;
> Seal it for Thy courts above.[8]

Consider This: (For Group Discussion)

1. How are knowledge and self-control related?

2. Share your highlights from studying Galatians 5:16. Especially focus on what you grew to understand and how you will apply this verse to your life.

3. Which of the four suggestions mentioned after the verse study do you most identify with as where God would have you grow? And why?

4. In what situations is it easy to ask God for strength and when is it hard and why?

---

8. Robert Robinson, Public Domain

The Next Step

5. Where should emotions play a part in our worship? How do they play a part in your worship?

6. On a personal note: In which area of your life do you especially need growth in self-control? Who could you share this with for encouragement and prayer?

CHAPTER 8

God as All-Powerful

When I think of the character quality of self-control, I think of personal strength to make the right decision, especially when I'm tempted to do what I want. Strength or power is needed. The corresponding attribute to God is that He is all-powerful. He really can do anything. When we look at a definition of God being all-powerful or His omnipotence, we read that "God's omnipotence means that God is able to do all his holy will."[1]

We saw in the last chapter how having self-control really means that we are controlled by God's Spirit; therefore, looking at God's omnipotence is very relevant.

Start your time with the Lord in prayer, asking God to strengthen you with His power, as Paul mentions in his prayer for the Colossians in Colossians 1:9–12:

> For this reason also, since the day we heard of it, we have not ceased to pray for you and to ask that you may be filled with the knowledge of His will in all spiritual wisdom and understanding, so that you will walk in a manner worthy of the Lord, to please Him in all respects, bearing fruit in every good work and increasing in the knowledge of God; strengthened with all power, according to His glorious might, for the attaining of all steadfastness and patience; joyously giving thanks to the Father, who has qualified us to share in the inheritance of the saints in Light.

---

1. Grudem, *Systematic Theology*, 216.

The Next Step

> To the Disciple: Our weaknesses make way for God's strength because we finally lay our pride aside and trust in the one who is all-powerful and He is for us (Romans 8:31). That is why humility is so important.

Now, read Isaiah 40:27–31:

> Why do you say, O Jacob, and assert, O Israel, 'my way is hidden from the Lord, and the justice due me escapes the notice of my God'? Do you not know? Have you not heard? The everlasting God, the Lord, the creator of the ends of the earth does not become weary or tired. His understanding is inscrutable. He gives strength to the weary, and to him who lacks might He increases power. Though youths grow weary and tired, and vigorous young men stumble badly, yet those who wait for the Lord will gain new strength; they will mount up with wings like eagles, they will run and not get tired, they will walk and not become weary.

- Have you felt the way this person felt as he begins this section?

- Can you remember a time when God strengthened you? What happened?

Next, copy Isaiah 40:31 onto a 3-by-5 card for your next verse to memorize and study in the verse study section. Keep it with your other cards and review them now. Keep working on memorizing these verses and review them daily. Keep handing the Holy Spirit these tools to use in your life.

God as All-Powerful

> To the Discipler: Pray for God to strengthen you to faithfully shepherd those you disciple, and pray for them to wait on the Lord to gain new strength, God's strength. Then pray with them through Isaiah 40:31.

Journaling

Hang in there. As you write down what God has been speaking to you from His word, you will often see a trend over time. This can show you an area God wants you to work on or give to Him.

Verse Study

Isaiah 40:31 is key to growing in self-control, but be sure to study this verse, not just for what you and I get out of this, but to better understand our great God.

Verse: Isaiah 40:31

Context:

Who is speaking? Who is the audience? What is the subject? What is the time frame, beginning and ending thought?

Key Words:

In light of the definitions, how do they expand or highlight this verse for me?

The Next Step

Cross References:

Verses that support my understanding of this verse.

For Discussion:

- What is the main issue being addressed here?

- What about this verse is challenging for me to believe?

- What sinful thinking or behavior does this verse expose in me?

- What would applying this truth in my life look like?

- How can we encourage one another in the truth of this verse?

God really is all-powerful. The English word "power" is used over 100 times in the Old Testament and even more in the New. Here is a sampling of verses addressing God's power:

- "Is anything too difficult for the Lord? At the appointed time I will return to you, at this time next year, and Sarah shall have a son." (Genesis 18:14, related to God's promise to Sarah to have a child in her old age.)
- "Ah Lord God! Behold, You have made the heavens and the earth by Your great power and by Your outstretched arm. Nothing is too difficult for You." (Jeremiah 32:17)
- "And looking at them Jesus said to them, 'With people this is impossible, but with God all things are possible.'" (Matthew 19:26, where Christ is answering the question, "Then who can be saved?")
- "Now to Him who is able to do far more abundantly beyond all that we ask or think, according to the power that works within us, to Him be the glory in the church and in Christ Jesus to all generations forever and ever. Amen." (Ephesians 3:20)
- "Who (the Lord Jesus Christ) will transform the body of our humble state into conformity with the body of His glory, by the exertion of the power that He has even to subject all things to Himself." (Philippians 3:21)

> "However, there are some things that God cannot do. God cannot will or do anything that would deny His own character. This is why the definition of omnipotence is stated in terms of God's ability to do "all his holy will."[2]

God is always consistent with His character. When He acts toward us, not only is all power available to Him — or, as Paul says in Philippians 3:21, "all things are subject to Him" — but His actions are loving and merciful and holy and just. They also take into account His omniscience, that He knows all things.

As an example, when we pray, we can be assured that God can do anything in answer to our prayers, and His answer will be in line with His love and compassion toward us. His answer will also take into account every possible consequence to that answer. His answer will be consistent with His holiness and righteousness. His answer will also be consistent

---

2. Grudem, *Systematic Theology*, 217.

with His working out His overall plans for all the earth. All of this together builds trust on our part and is part of the idea that God is trustworthy and glorious.

As you read God's word and come across an attribute of God, relate it to His other attributes. Ask Him to show you how this all connects in Him and then study the Bible to see those connections.

One example of this is related to Ephesians 3:20, mentioned above. Just before this verse that assures us God can do far beyond what we ask or think, Paul shares his desire for us to know the love of Christ which surpasses our knowledge. In one small section Paul writes about God's love, knowledge and power, and relates them all.

> To the Disciple: Remember: The powerful hand of God is always connected to His limitless heart and infinite mind.

What about grace?

So where does grace fit into the power of God? Look back at Jeremiah 32:17 and see what other attribute is addressed in that context and how it relates to His power. Jeremiah follows the verse on "Nothing Is Too Difficult for You" with "who shows lovingkindness to thousands, but repays the iniquity of fathers into the bosom of their children after them, O great and mighty God."

The Bible is clear that God's powerful hand is guided by His love and grace toward those who humbly turn to Him, but He will hold accountable those who refuse to humble themselves before Him and repent.

James sums this up wonderfully in James 4:6: "But He gives a greater grace. Therefore it says, 'God is opposed to the proud, but gives grace to the humble.'"

Ministry Skills: "8 to 15"

As you work on this section, you will not always remember to pray for your 8 to 15. I'm still working on that habit myself. So, what are some ways we can set aside some time and remember to pray for the 8 to 15 God put in each of our lives?

1. Put my list by my first task of the day—to make a pot of coffee.

2. Review the names when I first get into my car for the trip to work and then pray for them as I drive in.
3. Tape my list to my computer screen. (We look at that every day.)
4. Tie it in with another daily habit. I usually take a 20-minute walk to pray every morning. This would be a good spot for me.
5. (Your idea)

6. (Your idea)

Again, let me encourage you to visit 8to15.com and listen to Tom Mercer's heart. He will encourage you as you grow in reaching out to your "8 to 15."

> To the Disciple: One reason we pray is to place on our heart what is on God's heart. God will respond to our prayers for others by working in them, and He will also respond to our prayers for others by giving us His heart for them. (This is the point of Psalm 37:4.)

> To the Discipler: The same is true in us as we pray for those we're discipling. As we pray for them, God will work in their hearts to apply His word, and God will work in our hearts to have His love for them.

Personal Worship

"God has revealed Himself to us in His Word of truth and supremely in His Son, who is the truth (John 1:18; 14:6; 17;17). To worship God in truth means that we worship Him for all that He is in the majesty of His attributes as revealed in all of Scripture. We worship Him for His love, but also for His justice and righteousness. We worship Him for His kindness, but also for His severity (Romans 11:22). We worship Him for His sovereignty and for His grace. We worship Him when He gives, but also when He takes away (Job 1:20–21). We worship Him for all His ways."[3]

Here are two songs that help us reflect and meditate on the mighty power of God:

"I Stand in Awe"

You are beautiful beyond description
Too marvelous for words
Too wonderful of comprehension
Like nothing ever seen or heard
Who can grasp you infinite wisdom
Who can fathom the depth of your love
You are beautiful beyond description
Majesty enthroned above

And I stand, I stand in awe of you
I stand, I stand in awe of you
Holy God to whom all praise is due
I stand in awe of you.[4]

"How Great Thou Art"

O Lord my God, When I in awesome wonder
Consider all the worlds Thy Hands have made
I see the stars, I hear the rolling thunder
Thy power throughout the universe displayed

Chorus
Then sings my soul, My Savior God, to Thee
How great Thou art, How great Thou art
Then sings my soul, My Savior God, to Thee
How great Thou art, How great Thou art!

When through the woods, and forest glades I wander
And hear the birds sing sweetly in the trees
When I look down, from lofty mountain grandeur

---

3. Cole, "True Worship," 6.
4. Mark Altrogge (Sovereign Grace Praise, 2012).

God as All-Powerful

And see the brook, and feel the gentle breeze

Chorus

And when I think, that God, His Son not sparing
Sent Him to die, I scarce can take it in
That on the Cross, my burden gladly bearing
He bled and died to take away my sin

Chorus

When Christ shall come, with shout of acclamation
And take me home, what joy shall fill my heart
Then I shall bow, in humble adoration
And then proclaim: "My God, how great Thou art!"[5]

Consider This: (For Group Discussion)

1. What are some of the images that come to your mind when you hear the phrase "God is all-powerful"?

2. Share from your verse study of Isaiah 40:31. Was there anything new that you grew to understand?

3. What can you do this next month to grow in your understanding or awareness of God's power?

---

5. Stuart K. Hine (The Stuart Hine Trust, 1949, 1953, 2013).

The Next Step

4. How can we be just as confident in God being all-powerful when He doesn't answer our requests the way we want as when He does answer them the way we want?

5. How does God being the "Lord of Creation" affect your trust in bringing requests to Him? How else do we show we trust in God, other than prayer requests?

6. What Old Testament story gives you a clear picture of God's power?

CHAPTER 9

Perseverance

The character quality we are to add to Self-Control is *Perseverance*.

"Keep it up," "don't give up," "don't slow down," "you can do it." I remember hearing all of these "encouragements" when I ran track and cross country. My college coach and fellow runners were encouraging me to persevere in my workout or race. When I think back on those runs, they usually started with enthusiasm and expectations. They were long enough that I was tempted to slow down or even give up and stop.

As believers, we often begin with excitement and enthusiasm, but we need perseverance, because the Christian life is more of a long run than a sprint. This is especially applicable when we think of supplying perseverance to self-control. Whether it's self-control as related to temptations or to keeping up a new spiritual discipline like memorizing verses, I need the quality of perseverance to finish well.

Start your time with the Lord in prayer, looking at Luke 22:31–32 as an example, as the Lord prayed for Simon Peter:

> Simon, Simon, behold, Satan has demanded permission to sift you like wheat; but I have prayed for you that your faith may not fail; and you, when once you have turned again, strengthen your brothers.

When I read this I am reminded and motivated to pray that my faith will not fail and that I would be strengthened, and to remember that this strength comes from the Lord.

The Next Step

> To the Disciple: Stay the course. A runner will not see the finish line unless he or she finishes. We will see God's strength in us as we persevere.

Often the Psalmist is asking God for help to persevere. Psalm 138:7–8 is one example of this: "Though I walk in the midst of trouble, You will revive me; You will stretch forth Your hand against the wrath of my enemies, and Your right hand will save me. The Lord will accomplish what concerns me; Your lovingkindness, O Lord, is everlasting; do not forsake the works of Your hands."

What can you take away from these verses as encouragement?

Next, copy I Corinthians 15:58 onto a 3-by-5 card for your next verse to memorize and study in the verse study section. Keep it with your other cards and review them now. Keep working on memorizing these verses and review them daily. Keep handing the Holy Spirit these tools to use in your life.

> To the Discipler: Keep alert for signs of giving up in those with whom you meet. Send words of encouragement through phone calls, texts and emails. Change things up periodically and get together individually with them to reinforce your care. Let them know you're there for them.

Journaling

Take a few minutes and write in the journal section what God has been teaching you. Sometimes it helps to imagine it as writing a letter to God, responding to something He has taught you.

Perseverance

Verse Study

In I Corinthians 15:58, Paul exhorts us to persevere, especially in our work for the Lord. I hope this verse encourages you to "keep at it," "don't give up" and "hang in there."

Verse:

Context: (Who is speaking? Who is the audience? What is the subject? What is the time frame, beginning and ending thought?)

Key Words:

In light of the definitions, how do they expand or highlight this verse for me?

Cross References: (Verses that support my understanding of this verse)

For Discussion:

- What is the main issue being addressed here?

The Next Step

- What about this verse is challenging for me to believe?

- What sinful thinking or behavior does this verse expose in me?

- What would applying this truth in my life look like?

- How can we encourage one another in the truth of this verse?

Here are some consequences when we persevere:
1. As we grow in perseverance, we are perfected and completed as Christ's disciples, lacking in nothing (James 1:2–4).
2. We grow in confidence related to God's working in and through us (Philippians 1:6). This also includes becoming regular participants in the gospel.
3. Continuing in the Word leads to being Christ's disciple and knowing the truth which will set us free (John 8:31).
4. Persevering in love and obedience leads to God disclosing Himself to us (John 14:21).
5. Perseverance in abiding in Christ leads to much fruit (John 15:4–9).
6. Perseverance leads to growing in the fruit of the spirit (Galatians 6:9).

A passage that has helped me persevere, both with motivation and some how-tos, is Hebrews 12:1–3:

Perseverance

> Therefore, since we have so great a cloud of witnesses surrounding us, let us also lay aside every encumbrance and the sin which so easily entangles us, and let us run with endurance the race that is set before us, fixing our eyes on Jesus, the author and perfecter of faith, who for the joy set before Him endured the cross, despising the shame, and has sat down at the right hand of the throne of God. For consider Him who has endured such hostility by sinners against Himself, so that you will not grow weary and lose heart.

- Part of persevering is consciously laying aside things that slow me down or distract me in my Christian walk. When I ran track, I wore light clothes and running shoes. There are many things in life — some aren't even bad — that can distract me from walking with Christ. TVs and computers can distract us. Sports and recreation can. While I enjoy all of these, and I'm not saying to get rid of them, but you may need to set them aside if they distract you from focusing on the Lord. I regularly ask myself, "Do any of these take me away from walking with the Lord and serving Him?" When the answer is yes, I lay them aside.

- Another help for me from these verses is the exhortation to fix my eyes on Jesus, the author and perfecter of my faith. One of my main goals and desires in my daily quiet time with the Lord is to begin my day fixing my eyes on Him, to focus on the Lord, to gaze upon Him and let Him speak to me and lead me into my day. Then I pray for my eyes to stay on Him.

- Finally, this passage reminds me to consider Christ and the cross. Christ showed me how to persevere and to finish well. He did not grow weary or lose heart. As I tend at times to grow weary and lose my heart, I look to Christ and His finished work on the cross for me.

> To the Disciple: Philippians 3:13 reminds me that I can always have a fresh start with God. "Forgetting what lies behind and reaching forward to what lies ahead."

What about grace?

A verse that addresses perseverance over several generations is 2 Timothy 2:2: "The things which you have heard from me in the presence of many witnesses, entrust these to faithful men who will be able to teach others also." It speaks of passing these truths on and being faithful. I find it interesting that just prior to this exhortation, Paul wrote to Timothy, "You therefore my son, be strong in the grace that is in Christ Jesus" (2 Timothy 2:1).

I think Paul was telling Timothy to get all the grace he could from Christ, and also to ask for grace that he could give to others. We need God's grace to persevere and we need God's grace to help others persevere.

Ministry Skills: "8 to 15"

In Ecclesiastes 3:11 we read, "He has made everything appropriate in its time. He has also set eternity in their heart." Do I believe that everyone around me is thinking about eternity, or at least thinking about it at times? Do I believe that the people I run into every day are wrestling with the same questions I wrestled with as God drew me to Himself? I often look at those around me and conclude that they really have no interest in spiritual things or in God. That is not what the Bible says, and only God knows their hearts.

Would you pray differently for your 8 to 15 if you knew half or more of them were thinking about eternity and had questions about God? It would make a difference for me. I would say that everyone on your list is thinking about those things, and that is why God put them into your life.

Chew on that thought as you pray for your God-designed friendships, and look at 8to15.com again to listen to Tom Mercer's heart.

> To the Discipler: Could you answer these questions related to those you meet with: Where did they grow up? How did they become a Christian? What would they like to see God do in their lives this year? What is their biggest question about God? Go ahead, ask them.

Personal Worship

I'll take all the help I can get when it comes to thinking about the Lord throughout the day. At the end of my time in seminary, my wife and I spent a summer in Haiti. Often, during the week, as we worked alongside some Haitian believers, they would sing worship songs from Sunday. Sometimes

I found myself singing along. What a great help in fixing my eyes on Jesus, especially as the words of the song were often right out of the Bible.

Keep up your times of personal worship. Carry these songs with you as you go about your day. You might even search for these songs on line and listen to them. For growing in *Perseverance*, I've included these two songs:

"It Is Well with My Soul"

When peace, like a river, attendeth my way,
When sorrows like sea billows roll;
Whatever my lot, Thou has taught me to say,
It is well, it is well, with my soul.

It is well, with my soul,
It is well, it is well, with my soul.

Though Satan should buffet, though trials should come,
Let this blest assurance control,
That Christ has regarded my helpless estate,
And hath shed His own blood for my soul.

My sin, oh, the bliss of this glorious thought!
My sin, not in part but the whole,
Is nailed to the cross, and I bear it no more,
Praise the Lord, praise the Lord, O my soul!

For me, be it Christ, be it Christ hence to live:
If Jordan above me shall roll,
No pang shall be mine, for in death as in life
Thou wilt whisper Thy peace to my soul.

But, Lord, 'tis for Thee, for Thy coming we wait,
The sky, not the grave, is our goal;
Oh, trump of the angel! Oh, voice of the Lord!
Blessed hope, blessed rest of my soul!

And Lord, haste the day when my faith shall be sight,
The clouds be rolled back as a scroll;
The trump shall resound, and the Lord shall descend,
Even so, it is well with my soul.[1]

---

1. Horatio G. Spafford, Public Domain.

The Next Step

"You Are My Hiding Place"

You are my hiding place
You always fill my heart
With songs of deliverance
Whenever I am afraid I will trust in You

I will trust in You
Let the weak say I am strong
In the strength of the Lord

You are my hiding place
You always fill my heart
With songs of deliverance
Whenever I am afraid I will trust in You

I will trust in You
Let the weak say I am strong
In the strength of the Lord
I will trust in You[2]

Consider This: (For Group Discussion)

1. Give an example from your life where someone encouraged you to persevere in something, where they made a difference in you not giving up? How did they help you?

2. Review the verse study of I Corinthians 15:58, highlighting what God taught you about persevering.

---

2. Michael James Ledner (Universal Music—Brentwood Benson Publ., 1993).

Perseverance

3. Give a biblical example of someone who persevered. Now give a present-day example of someone who is persevering and an encouragement to you.

4. What distractions in your life do you need to lay aside in order to better fix your eyes on Jesus?

5. If a young believer asked you for help in how they could grow in focusing more on Christ, what would you tell them?

6. What was the most practical thing you took away from this chapter on perseverance this week?

Chapter 10

God as Sovereign

Looking at the sovereignty of God is probably the most encouraging study you or I could do. This is especially true as you keep in mind all of God's attributes. Wayne Grudem defines God's sovereignty as "His exercise of rule (as 'sovereign' or 'king') over his creation."[1] As proclaimed in Deuteronomy 4:39, "Know therefore today, and take it to your heart, that the Lord, He is God in heaven above and on the earth below; there is no other."

In the Old Testament times, Israel seemed to be more concerned in their animal sacrifices than in giving God their hearts, so the Psalmist writes this in Psalm 50:10–15:

> For every beast of the forest is Mine, the cattle on a thousand hills. I know every bird of the mountains, and everything that moves in the field is Mine. If I were hungry I would not tell you, for the world is Mine, and all it contains. Shall I eat the flesh of bulls or drink the blood of males goats? Offer to God a sacrifice of thanksgiving and pay our vows to the Most High; call upon Me in the day of trouble; I shall rescue you, and you will honor Me.

As you reflect on a sovereign God who owns everything, what would He have you give Him today? Express that to the Lord in prayer.

> To the Disciple: A daily God-hunt, where I look for God at work around me, helps me to see His hand at work.

---

1. Grudem, *Systematic Theology*, 217.

God as Sovereign

Now, read Psalm 24:1–10:

> The earth is the Lord's, and all it contains, the world, and those who dwell in it. For He has founded it upon the seas and established it upon the rivers. Who may ascend into the hill of the Lord? And who may stand in His holy place? He who has clean hands and a pure heart, who has not lifted up his soul to falsehood and has not sworn deceitfully. He shall receive a blessing from the Lord and righteousness from the God of his salvation. This is the generation of those who seek Him, who seek Your face, even Jacob. Lift up your heads, O gates, and be lifted up, O ancient doors, that the King of glory may come in. Who is the King of glory? The Lord strong and mighty, the Lord mighty in battle. Lift up your heads, O gates, and lift them up, O ancient doors, that the King of glory may come in. Who is this King of glory? The Lord of hosts, He is the King of glory.

- What does this Psalm tell you about our God?

- How can you respond to Him as we begin this chapter on His sovereignty?

Next, copy Romans 8:28 onto a 3-by-5 card for your next verse to memorize and study in the verse study section. Take a few minutes now to review your other verses. As you review, ask God to show you what that verse means and how it relates to your life this day.

> To the Discipler: To help those you meet with see God in everyday situations, share how you have seen God at work in your life this past week.

The Next Step

Journaling

As the Lord teaches you throughout the week, go to the back of this book and write down what you've learned.

Verse Study

Romans 8:28 brings the idea of God's sovereignty right into our laps. This is many people's favorite verse, and you will see why in this study.

Verse:

Context:

Who is speaking? Who is the audience? What is the subject? What is the time frame, beginning and ending thought?

Key Words:

In light of the definitions, how do they expand or highlight this verse for me?

Cross References:

Verses that support my understanding of this verse.

God as Sovereign

For Discussion:

- What is the main issue being addressed here?

- What about this verse is challenging for me to believe?

- What sinful thinking or behavior does this verse expose in me?

- What would applying this truth in my life look like?

- How can we encourage one another in the truth of this verse?

God's Sovereignty is seen is several areas:
1. God's sovereignty is seen in His hand in world affairs:

    Daniel said, Let the name of God be blessed forever and ever, for wisdom and power belong to Him. It is He who changes the times and the epochs; He removes kings and establishes kings; He gives wisdom to wise men and knowledge to men of understanding." (Daniel 2:20–21; see also 2 Chronicles 20:6, Psalm 75:6,7 and Isaiah 40:22–23)

2. God's sovereignty is seen in all creation being created by Him and belonging to Him.

> Yours, O Lord, is the greatness and the power and the glory and the victory and the majesty, indeed everything that is in the heavens and the earth; Yours is the dominion, O Lord, and You exalt Yourself as head over all. Both riches and honor come from You, and You rule over all, and in Your hand is power and might; and it lies in Your hand to make great and to strengthen everyone." (2 Chronicles 29:11–12)

> Who has given to Me that I should repay him? Whatever is under the whole heaven is Mine." (Job 41:11; see also Job 12:154, Psalm 89:11 and Psalm 135:5)

Keep in mind that all of God's creation exists for His pleasure and God is most pleased when we enjoy Him.[2]

"Worthy are You, our Lord and our God, to receive glory and honor and power; for You created all things, and because of Your will they existed, and were created" (Revelation 4:11).

3. God is sovereign over all the circumstances of our lives, good and bad.

> "Who among all these does not know that the hand of the Lord has done this, in whose hand is the life of every living thing, and the breath of all mankind?" (Job 12:9; see also Acts 17:24-26)

4. God's sovereignty is seen in the resolution of salvation throughout world history: "God's sovereignty is expressed, exercised and displayed in the divine plan for and outworking of salvation history."[3]

> "But when the fullness of the time came, God sent forth His Son, born of a woman, born under the Law, so that He might redeem those who were under the Law, that we might receive the adoption as sons." (Galatians 4:4, 5; see also Ephesians 1:10-11)

5. God's sovereignty is related to His choosing me to be His child by His grace.

> Blessed be the God and Father of our Lord Jesus Christ, who has blessed us with every spiritual blessing in the heavenly places in

---

2. Piper, *Desiring God*.
3. Grenz et al., *Pocket Dictionary*, 109.

God as Sovereign

Christ, just as He chose us in Him before the foundation of the world, that we would be holy and blameless before Him. In love He predestined us to adoption as sons through Jesus Christ to Himself, according to the kind intention of His will, to the praise of the glory of His grace, which He freely bestowed on us in the Beloved." (Ephesians 1:3-6)

Note: Let me address the tension we sometimes have with God's sovereignty and man's responsibility. J.I. Packer's *Evangelism and the Sovereignty of God* has helped me with this: "God's sovereignty and man's responsibility are taught us side by side in the same Bible; sometimes, indeed, in the same text (I.e. Acts 2:23). Both are thus guaranteed to us by the same divine authority; both, therefore, are true. It follows that they must be held together, and not played off against each other. Man is a responsible moral agent, though he is also divinely controlled; man is divinely controlled, though he is also a responsible moral agent. God's sovereignty is a reality, and man's responsibility is a reality too. This is the revealed antinomy in terms of which we have to do our thinking about evangelism."[4]

Let me leave you with four implications:

- We must respond to God's call to Himself. "But as many as received Him, to them He gave the right to become children of God, even to those who believe in His name." (John 1:12)
- We give Him all the credit for saving us as a free gift by faith alone and take no credit in earning His favor (Ephesians 2:8, 9).
- We must tell others about salvation so that they can respond in faith (Romans 10:14, 15).
- I am eternally grateful for God's grace toward me in choosing me.

> To the Disciple: I understand God's grace to the degree that I extend grace to others. Ephesians 4:32 is a good test for my understanding God's forgiveness and, therefore, grace to me. "Be kind to one another, tender-hearted, forgiving each other, just as God in Christ also has forgiven you."

---

4. Packer, *Evangelism and the Sovereignty of God*, 22.

The Next Step

What about grace?

Studying the sovereignty of God pushes me to another degree in understanding God's grace. As Romans 5:6–8 states: "For while we were still helpless, at the right time Christ died for the ungodly. For one will hardly die for a righteous man; though perhaps for the good man someone would dare even to die. But God demonstrates His own love toward us, in that while we were yet sinners, Christ died for us." Paul goes on to state that God did this reconciling while we were enemies.

In verse 2 of the same chapter, Paul tells us that this justification, or having peace with God, is our introduction by faith into God's grace. This is just the introduction? Grace is pretty amazing!

Ministry Skills: "8 to 15"

The mission statement at Tom Mercer's High Desert Church declares, "We exist solely to prepare every generation to change their worlds for Christ."[5] If every believer in your town prayed regularly for their 8 to 15 divinely placed friends, family members and acquaintances, most everyone in your city would probably be covered. God would be working in their hearts to draw them to Him, and as you and I looked for opportunities to engage with them, we would see change, and some of them would come to know Christ as their savior.

Don't miss out on an opportunity to change your world for Christ. And remember: God is not asking you to pray for and reach out to the whole world, just the 8 to 15 He has brought into your life. The world is smaller than you think.

> To the Disciple: Christ often used questions to engage with those who came to Him. Learn the art of asking good questions.

---

5. Mercer, *8 to 15*, 52.

God as Sovereign

> To the Discipler: Ask those with whom you're meeting if they have someone they can share their learning with. Sharing lessons with someone else will cement them even more in your life.

Personal Worship

Here are two songs to help us reflect and meditate on the sovereignty of God. Let me encourage you to search for these songs online and listen to them now and then, especially if you don't remember the tune. Listening can help us personally praise the Lord, and you will be encouraged and lifted up as you listen and sing along.

"Sovereign Over Us"

There is strength within the sorrow, There is beauty in our tears
You meet us in our mourning, With a love that casts out fear
You are working in our waiting, Sanctifying us
When beyond our understanding, You're teaching us to trust

CHORUS

Your plans are still to prosper, You have not forgotten us
You're with us in the fire and the flood
Faithful forever, Perfect in love
You are sovereign over us

You are wisdom unimagined, Who could understand your ways
Reigning high above the heavens, Reaching down in endless grace
You're the Lifter of the lowly, Compassionate and kind
You surround and You uphold me, Your promises are my delight

Even what the enemy means for evil
You turn it for our good, You turn it for our good and for your glory
Even in the valley You are faithful
You're working for our good, You're working for our good and for your glory[6]

"How Great Thou Art"

O Lord my God, When I in awesome wonder,
Consider all the worlds Thy Hands have made;

---

6. Aaron Keyes, Bryan Brown and Jack Mooring (Thankyou Music, 2011).

The Next Step

> I see the stars, I hear the rolling thunder,
> Thy power throughout the universe displayed.
>
> Then sings my soul, My Savior God, to Thee,
> How great Thou art, How great Thou art.
> Then sings my soul, My Savior God, to Thee,
> How great Thou art, How great Thou art!
>
> When through the woods, and forest glades I wander,
> And hear the birds sing sweetly in the trees.
> When I look down, from lofty mountain grandeur
> And see the brook, and feel the gentle breeze.
>
> And when I think, that God, His Son not sparing;
> Sent Him to die, I scarce can take it in;
> That on the Cross, my burden gladly bearing,
> He bled and died to take away my sin.
>
> When Christ shall come, with shout of acclamation,
> And take me home, what joy shall fill my heart.
> Then I shall bow, in humble adoration,
> And then proclaim: "My God, how great Thou art!"[7]

Consider This: (For Group Discussion)

1. Provide an example of seeing God's hand at work in the world around you.

2. Review your study of Romans 8:28, highlighting what you've learned about God and how it applies to your life.

---

7. Stuart K. Hine (The Stuart Hine Trust, 1949, 1953, 2013).

God as Sovereign

3. How do you recognize God's sovereignty in world affairs?

4. If God is sovereign over the circumstances of your life, how should this affect your response to those circumstances, both good and bad?

5. What is encouraging about studying God's sovereignty and what is difficult about it?

6. Reflect on the worship songs and choose one phrase you find especially encouraging.

CHAPTER 11

Godliness

The fifth virtue in our list of virtues to add to our faith from 2 Peter 1:5-7, is Godliness. The word used here is *eusebeian*, which comes from *eu*, meaning "well," and *seboma*, meaning to be devout[1]. Godliness is piety or devotion to the person of God. Michael Green, in his commentary on 2 Peter, defines it as "a very practical awareness of God in every aspect of life."[2]

"To be godly is to live reverently, loyally, and obediently toward God."[3]

Worked out in everyday life, someone with the virtue of godliness has his or her attention directed toward God. He or she recognizes God's personal attention that David addresses in Psalm 139. There is nowhere we can go that God does not see us. They also desire to know and please God in every circumstance, recognizing God's hand in every circumstance they live in, and use that circumstance to please and glorify God.

Start your time with the Lord in prayer by looking at Ephesians 1:15-19. Included in this prayer is an awareness of God's working in our lives:

> For this reason I too, having heard of the faith in the Lord Jesus which exists among you and your love for all the saints, do not cease giving thanks for you, while making mention of you in my prayers; that the God of our Lord Jesus Christ, the Father of glory, may give to you a spirit of wisdom and of revelation in the knowledge of Him. I pray that the eyes of your heart may be enlightened, so that you will know what is the hope of His calling, what are the

1. Vine et al, *Vine's Complete Expository Dictionary*, 272.
2. Green, *New Testament Commentaries*, 70.
3. MacArthur, *The MacArthur Study Bible*, 1952.

Godliness

riches of the glory of His inheritance in the saints, and what is the surpassing greatness of His power toward us who believe.

The hope of His calling, the riches of His inheritance and the surpassing greatness of His power toward us is a 24/7 reality. What I mean by this is that God's attention toward us for our good in each of these areas happens every hour of every day. Meditate upon that thought.

> To the Disciple: Being aware of God in every aspect of our lives begins with understanding His attitude about us and desires for us. Each prayer in the Bible is a window into God's heart.

Psalm 23 gives us a wonderful picture of God's involvement in every part of our lives:

> The Lord is my shepherd, I shall not want. He makes me lie down in green pastures; He leads me beside quiet waters. He restores my soul; He guides me in the paths of righteousness for His name's sake. Even though I walk through the valley of the shadow of death, I fear no evil, for You are with me; Your rod and Your staff, they comfort me. You prepare a table before me in the presence of my enemies; You have a anointed my head with oil; my cup overflows. Surely goodness and lovingkindness will follow me all the days of my life, and I will dwell in the house of the Lord forever."

- What is the Psalmist's attitude about God's attention to him?

- How do you feel about God's attention toward you?

Next, write 1 Timothy 4:7,8 onto a 3-by-5 card for your next verse to memorize and study in the verse study section. Keep it with your other cards and review them now. Keep working on memorizing these verses and

The Next Step

review them daily. Keep handing the Holy Spirit these tools to use in your life.

> To the Discipler: The key to memorizing scripture is daily review. Someone once told me that if you review a verse every day for six weeks, you will never forget that verse. I have tested this and found it to be true!

Journaling

Go to the Journaling section in the back of this book and write down something God has taught you in this lesson so far and respond to God with a prayer.

Verse Study

In 1 Timothy 4:7, 8, Paul challenges us to evaluate what receives our attention. As you study these two verses, wrestle with how Godliness is profitable for all things in your life.

Verse: I Timothy 4:7, 8

Context:

Who is speaking? Who is the audience? What is the subject? What is the time frame, beginning and ending thought?

Key Words:

In light of the definitions, how do they expand or highlight this verse for me?

Cross References:

Verses that support my understanding of this verse.

For Discussion:

- What is the main issue being addressed here?

- What about this verse is challenging for me to believe?

- What sinful thinking or behavior does this verse expose in me?

The Next Step

- What would applying this truth in my life look like?

- How can we encourage one another in the truth of this verse?

> To the Disciple: Understanding God's graciousness toward me increases my view of God and lessens my view of myself (John 3:30). (This would be true of every attribute of God.)

As I address the quality of Godliness here, three truths help me grow:

1. I find that it helps *to realize that God is very present in every detail of my life.* He is always with me. Looking back to Psalm 139, in verses 2 to 5 David writes, "You know when I sit down and when I rise up; you understand my thought from afar, you scrutinize my path and my lying down, and are intimately acquainted with all my ways. Even before there is a word on my tongue, behold O Lord, You know it all. You have enclosed me behind and before, and laid your hand upon me."

Four things about God's attention toward us stand out in these verses:

- God's awareness and attention is complete and always toward us.
- God understands all my thinking processes and reasoning.
- God can see ahead to the consequences of all my plans and actions.
- God's effective presence is always with me. His hand is always on me.

2. When I wrestle with the importance of Godliness being linked with contentment in 1 Timothy 6:6–8, I realize the importance of *a clear view of God's sovereign hand in all of my life.*

> But godliness actually is a means of great gain when accompanied by contentment. For we have brought nothing into the world, so we cannot take anything out of it either. If we have food and covering, with these we shall be content.

If Godliness is "a very practical awareness of God in every aspect of my life" and contentment is a satisfaction in the circumstances of one's life as we recognize God's hand as the source and director of those circumstances, then I grow in godliness and contentment as I grow in clearly seeing or believing that God is in control.

3. *Fixing my eyes on Jesus* as the author and "perfecter" of my faith helps me grow in Godliness. In 2 Peter 1:2,3 Peter writes to us, "Grace and peace be multiplied to you in the knowledge of God and of Jesus our Lord; seeing that His divine power has granted to us everything pertaining to life and godliness, through the true knowledge of Him who called us by His own glory and excellence."

God has given us what we need for life and godliness through the knowledge of Christ. I find that as I focus my mind and heart or affections on Christ I am captivated by Him. Colossians 2:3 tells me that in Christ "are hidden all the treasures of wisdom and knowledge." A few verses later (verse 8) Paul exhorts us to not be captivated by the world's philosophy or traditions, but implies that we should be captivated by Christ.

David tells me to be captivated and satisfied in the Lord in Psalm 37:4: "Delight yourself in the Lord and He will give you the desires of your heart." As I wrap my desires and pursuits with my delights and joys, and fix my eyes on Jesus, He brings them all together in Him and helps me live a Godly and Godward life.

What about grace?

We saw how grace and peace being multiplied to us is related to our growing in godliness in 2 Peter 1:2&3. In verse 4 we read how God has "granted to us His precious and magnificent promises" so that we might become partakers of the divine nature. The word "granted" speaks of God giving us this wonderful privilege. "Partakers of the divine nature" speaks of our growth in godliness. This is all by God's grace, undeserved on our part and reflective of God's gracious heart toward us.

Ministry Skills: "8 to 15"

As I worked on this chapter yesterday, God led one of my 8 to 15 to call me and pour his heart out. What a divine appointment. I was reminded to ask

The Next Step

God to help me expect this. He is working in lives, and some of those lives are the people for whom we pray.

Keep praying daily for your supernaturally designed friendships, and God will surprise you with a divine appointment.

> To the Discipler: Look for opportunities during the week to call someone you are meeting with and ask him or her to join you in a ministry, like a home visit or at a sporting event. Some of our best "discipling" can happen during casual times together.

Personal Worship

Feel free to sing and reflect on past songs along with these new ones as they relate to each week's topic. As often as possible meditate on these songs as you start your day. You can download many of these songs onto a tablet or smart phone and play them as you drive throughout the day.

For growing in *Godliness*, I've included these two songs:

"I Give You My Heart"

This is my desire: to honor You.
Lord with all my heart I worship You.
All I have within me, I give You praise.
All that I adore is in You.

Lord I give You my heart,
I give You my soul, I live for You alone.
Every breath that I take,
Every moment I'm awake,
Lord have Your way in me.

This is my desire: to honor You.
Lord with all my heart I worship You.
All I have within me, I give You praise.
All that I adore is in You.

Lord I give You my heart,
I give You my soul, I live for You alone.
Every breath that I take,
Every moment I'm awake,
Lord have Your way in me.[4]

---

4. Reuben Morgan (Hillsong Music Publishing, 1995).

"10,000 Reasons (Bless the Lord)"

Bless the lord oh my soul Oh my soul
Worship his holy name
Sing like never before Oh my soul
I worship your holy name

The sun comes up Its a new day dawning
It's time to sing your song again
What ever may pass and whatever lies before me
Let me be singing when the evening comes

Bless the lord oh my soul Oh my soul
Worship his holy name
Sing like never before Oh my soul
I worship your holy name

You're rich in love and you're slow to anger
Your name is great and your heart is kind
For all your goodness I will keep on singing
10,000 reasons for my heart to find

Bless the lord oh my soul Oh my soul
Worship his holy name
Sing like never before Oh my soul
I worship your holy name

And on that day when my strength is failing
The end draws near and my time has come
Soon my soul will sing your praise un-ending
10,000 years and there forever more

Bless the lord oh my soul Oh my soul
Worship his holy name
Sing like never before Oh my soul
I worship your holy name

Bless the lord oh my soul Oh my soul
Worship his holy name
Sing like never before Oh my soul
I worship your holy name
I worship your holy name
I worship your holy name

The Next Step

> Sing like never before Oh my soul
> I worship your holy name
> (Jesus I will)
> I worship your holy name
> I worship your holy name[5]

Consider This: (For Group Discussion)

1. When you think about the character quality of Godliness, who comes to your mind as an example and why?

2. Review the study of I Timothy 4: 7 and 8 and share what God taught you from these verses.

3. What is something new you learned about Godliness from this week's study?

4. What helps you to be more aware of God's presence in your life throughout the week?

---

5. Jonas Myrin, Matt Redman (Shout! Publishing, 2011).

5. What application can you take from this week's study to apply to your life this week?

6. How can the "Personal Worship" section at the end of each chapter help you grow in the quality of Godliness?

Chapter 12

The Holiness of God

"God's holiness means that he is separated from sin and devoted to seeking his own honor."[1]

Holiness has both the idea of a separation from evil and a devotion to God's own glory and honor.

In Jerry Bridges' *The Pursuit of Holiness*, we read: "God's holiness then is perfect freedom from all evil. We say a garment is clean when it is free from any spot, or gold is pure when all dross has been refined from it. In this manner we can think of the holiness of God as the absolute absence of any evil in Him."[2] In this chapter we will look further at the holiness of God, what it tells us about God, and the implications to us who are sinful even as we are given the privilege to walk with Him.

At the beginning of Isaiah's ministry, we read this in Isaiah 6:1–5:

> In the year of King Uzziah's death I saw the Lord sitting on a throne, lofty and exalted, with the train of His robe filling the temple. Seraphim stood above Him, each having six wings: with two he covered his face, and with two he covered his feet,, and with two he flew. And one called out to another and said, Holy, Holy, Holy, is the Lord of hosts, the whole earth is full of His glory. And the foundations of the thresholds trembled at the voice of him who called out, while the temple was filling with smoke. Then I said, "Woe is me, for I am ruined! Because I am a man of unclean lips, and I live among a people of unclean lips, for my eyes have seen the King, the Lord of hosts."

---

1. Grudem, *Systematic Theology*, 201.
2. Bridges, *The Pursuit of Holiness*, 26.

The Holiness of God

What do you think was going through Isaiah's mind as he saw the Lord?

As the prophet Nathan confronted him about his sin, David reflected on both the holiness of God and God's mercy in praying this prayer:

> Behold, You desire truth in the innermost being, and in the hidden part You will make me know wisdom. Purify me with hyssop, and I shall be clean; wash me, and I shall be whiter than snow. Make me to hear joy and gladness, let the bones which You have broken rejoice. Hide Your face from my sins and blot out all my iniquities. Create in me a clean heart, O God, and renew a steadfast spirit within me. Do not cast me away from Your presence and do not take Your Holy Spirit from me. Restore to me the joy of Your salvation and sustain me with a willing spirit. Then I will teach transgressors Your ways, and sinners will be converted to You. (Psalm 51:6–13)

- What does this prayer say about the holiness of God?

- What does this prayer say about the mercy of God?

> To the Disciple: Humility is what God desires from each of us and is not what we can do or contribute but a broken spirit; "A broken and a contrite heart, O God, You will not despise" (Psalm 51:17).

Next, copy 1 Peter 1:15,16 onto a 3-by-5 card for your next verse to memorize and study in the verse study section. Take a few minutes now to

The Next Step

review your other verses. As you review each verse ask God to show you what that verse means and how it relates to your life this day.

> To the Discipler: "Therefore there is now no condemnation for those who are in Christ Jesus" (Romans 8:1).

Journaling

Go to the back of this book and write down in the Journaling section something God has taught you in this lesson so far, and respond to God with a prayer.

Verse Study

Study 1 Peter 1:15,16, asking God to show you His holiness even as we are to be holy.

Verse: I Peter 1:15, 16

Context:

Who is speaking? Who is the audience? What is the subject? What is the time frame, beginning and ending thought?

Key Words:

In light of the definitions, how do they expand or highlight this verse for me?

Cross References:

Verses that support my understanding of this verse.

For Discussion:

- What is the main issue being addressed here?

- What about this verse is challenging for me to believe?

- What sinful thinking or behavior does this verse expose in me?

- What would applying this truth in my life look like?

- How can we encourage one another in the truth of this verse?

The Next Step

God's Holiness is both fearful and wonderful; What do I need to understand about God's holiness?

1. That I really do not grasp how holy holiness is. I begin attempting to understand this attribute of God somewhat stumped. I've already given you a definition at the beginning, but what can I say about God's holiness? "Holy" and "holiness" are very Christian, or "churchy," terms, used all the time, but do I understand them? I have a sense of right and wrong, but does this adequately address holiness? At times I grow in seeing my own sinfulness and unholiness before God, and in those times see a God who does no evil, but is holiness just an absence of evil? In a positive way is it not also the complete perfection of good? As far as that goes, does it not also relate to God's perfection in all of His attributes? God's holiness then would include His perfect compassion and mercy to me, a sinner. I do not understand this, but I am very grateful for it.

As I wrestle with understanding this, I have come to greatly appreciate the promise at the end of John 14:21: "He who has My commandments and keeps them is the one who loves Me; and he who loves Me will be loved by My Father, and I will love him and will disclose Myself to him." Lord, I need you to disclose yourself to me. Thank you for the promise that you will.

2. That in spite of the infinite difference between God and I related to holiness, He is working in me to make me holy. God commands us to be holy as stated in our memory verse; therefore, we can grow in holiness, by His grace and strength. Paul tells us in 2 Corinthians 5:21 that God "made Him (Christ) who knew no sin to be sin on our behalf, so that we might become the righteousness of God in Him."

In this verse we see how God can be consistent with all His attributes in justly making sinners righteous and thereby being able to spend eternity with Him. That is God's present work in every believer through the Holy Spirit in our lives (see also 1 Peter 3:18).

In Philippians 1:6, Paul addresses this also: "For I am confident of this very thing, that He who began a good work in you will perfect it until the day of Christ Jesus."

This is also what Paul is stating in Romans 8:1–4 when he proclaims that we who deserve to be condemned have no more condemnation.

> Therefore there is now no condemnation for those who are in Christ Jesus. For the law of the Spirit of life in Christ Jesus has set you free from the law of sin and of death. For what the Law could not do, weak as it was through the flesh, God did: sending His

The Holiness of God

own Son in the likeness of sinful flesh and as an offering for sin, He condemned sin in the flesh, so that the requirement of the Law might be fulfilled in us, who do not walk according to the flesh but according to the Spirit.

This is the amazing bringing together of God's holiness and righteousness, of His omnipotence and omniscience and mercy and love.

3. *That our becoming holy will bring us and God the greatest joy.* In Romans 14:17 we read, "For the kingdom of God is not eating and drinking, but righteousness and peace and joy in the Holy Spirit." Righteousness addresses my growing in holiness before God, both in terms of my sin paid for and being given the righteousness of Christ. Peace addresses a broken relationship with God because of my going my own way, being reconciled or resolved, restored. Joy is the result of being made right in every way with my creator who knows how to thrill us and give us the most joy.

Remember James 1:16–17: "Do not be deceived, my beloved brethren. Every good thing given and every perfect gift is from above, coming down from the Father of lights, with whom there is no variation or shifting shadow." Every perfect gift is from God and He made us so He knows what's perfect to us!

> To the Disciple: We don't naturally identify holiness with joy, but let me give you an analogy. After working all day in the peach orchard, I feel itchy, dirty, and generally lousy. Then, after a nice shower with shampoo and soap, I feel clean and refreshed and good! In the same way, as I live in the world and wrestle with sin and temptation, I come to the Lord for cleansing and forgiveness, and I feel good!

What about grace?

In Galatians 3:1–3 Paul wrote, "You foolish Galatians, who has bewitched you, before whose eyes Jesus Christ was publicly portrayed as crucified? This is the only thing I want to find out from you: did you receive the Spirit by the works of the Law, or by hearing with faith? Are you so foolish? Having begun by the Spirit, are you now being perfected by the flesh?" Paul is correcting the Galatian believers. There were some who recognized that salvation was a gift by faith, but then were taught that growth was by the law and of the flesh. Paul corrects this by stating that we also continue to grow by faith. Our becoming holy is God's work in us by faith and nothing we can boast in. It is a gift of God by His grace.

Ministry Skills: "8 to 15"

Tom Mercer gives this example in *8 to 15* of an act of kindness that led to a point of contact: "Do the unexpected. One of our members told me about rolling a trash can back up the driveway for his elderly neighbor because he knew it was a bit of a struggle for her. She didn't know he was doing that for several weeks, and then, one day, she finally saw it was him. That led to a conversation."[3] Tom went on to challenge us to "be yourself, be nice, be consistent, be persistent and listen to the voice of the Holy Spirit."[4]

> To the Disciple: The more we ask others, with genuine interest, questions about themselves, the better chance that they will ask us questions too. Keep it up and you will be asked why you do what you do.

> To the Discipler: When you ask questions, ask the Lord to give you insights into those you're discipling to delve further, learn more about them, and, sometimes, get to issues in their lives.

Personal Worship

Here are two songs that help us reflect and meditate on the holiness of God. Every attribute of God should cause a response in our hearts and minds. These can be responses of changed behavior, or responses of changed thinking, or just responses of verbal praise. Songs of praise and worship often help us with that response. As you reflect on these songs, look for ways you can respond to God for His amazing Holiness.

---

3. Mercer, *8 to 15*, 102.
4. Ibid.

"Holy Is The Lord"

We stand and lift up our hands
For the joy of the Lord is our strength
We bow down and worship Him now
How great, how awesome is He

And together we sing

[Chorus]
Holy is the Lord God Almighty
The earth is filled with His glory
Holy is the Lord God Almighty
The earth is filled with His glory
The earth is filled with His glory

We stand and lift up our hands
For the joy of the Lord is our strength
We bow down and worship Him now
How great, how awesome is He

And together we sing
Everyone sing

[Chorus]
Holy is the Lord God Almighty
The earth is filled with His glory
Holy is the Lord God Almighty
The earth is filled with His glory
The earth is filled with His glory

It's rising up all around
It's the anthem of the Lord's renown
Repeat

And together we sing,
Everyone sing[5]

---

5. Chris Tomlin, Louie Giglio (Worshiptogether.com songs and sixsteps Music, 2003).

The Next Step

"Great Are You Lord"

Holy Lord, most Holy Lord.
You alone are worthy of my praise
Oh Holy Lord, most Holy Lord
With all of my heart I sing

Great are you, Lord
Worthy of Praise
Holy and true
Great are you, Lord
Most Holy Lord[6]

Consider This: (For Group Discussion)

1. Review the study of I Peter 1:15 and 16 and note what God has taught you about being holy.

2. How is holiness related to godliness?

3. What is something new you learned about the holiness of God?

4. What should motivate us to be holy? What motivates you to give it your attention?

---

6. Stephen R. Cook, Vikki Anne Cook (Universal Music—Brentwood Benson Publishing, 1984).

5. What is your greatest obstacle to growing in holiness?

6. What part does worship play in our growing in holiness?

CHAPTER 13

Brotherly Kindness

The character quality we are to add to *Godliness* is *Brotherly Kindness*. The Greek word for this is *Philadelphian*, and it means "brotherly friendship," the love of the brethren. Philadelphian "denotes the warmth of affection that should characterize the fellowship of believers."[1]

This quality speaks of a depth of devotion beyond normal friendship. In Romans 12:10, Paul writes, "Be devoted to one another in brotherly love." When we say we are brothers and sisters in Christ we are speaking of family. In the same way that there is a stronger bond between members of the same physical family, there is also a stronger bond between believers, for we are together in God's family.

Start your time with the Lord in prayer, looking at John 13:34–35. So far, I've mainly given you prayers from the Bible to guide your prayer time. Commands we are given are also great to pray. When we are commanded something, we know that it's God's will, and when we pray, I find it helpful to be praying through these commands.

> A new commandment I give to you, that you love one another, even as I have loved you, that you also love one another. By this all men will know that you are My disciples, if you have love for one another.

- Are there brothers and/or sisters in Christ that are hard to love?

---

1. Gaebelein, *The Expositor's Bible Commentary*, 270.

Brotherly Kindness

- How can you be praying for them today along with your relationship with them, as you work through this study?

> To the Disciple: In Ephesians 6, where Paul tells us to put on the full armor of God, he talks about prayer but doesn't identify it with any armor. In this picture, prayer is the soldier fighting alongside you, watching your back. When we pray for other believers we're watching out for them.

In Ecclesiastes 4:9–12, Solomon addresses the value of having others in our lives to lift us up and strengthen us. As you read over these verses, relate them to the value of Christian family.

> Two are better than one because they have a good return for their labor. For if either of them falls, the one will lift up his companion. But woe to the one who falls when there is not another to lift him up. Furthermore, if two lie down together they keep warm, but how can one be warm alone? And if one can overpower him who is alone, two can resist him. A cord of three strands is not quickly torn apart.

- How have you seen this to be true in your Christian life?

- Who has God brought into your life to lift you up or strengthen you?

Next, copy Romans 12:10 onto a 3-by-5 card for your next verse to memorize and study in the verse study section. Have you found certain

The Next Step

times in your day that are the best to review these verses? Keep it up; it will become a habit, then a privilege.

> To the Discipler: Disciplining yourself to daily pray for those with whom you meet is a worthwhile habit to develop. Part of praying for them is to pray for a heart to pray for them.

Journaling

Go to the end of the book and write down in the Journaling section something God has taught you in this lesson so far and respond to God with a prayer.

Verse Study

In Romans 12:10, Paul challenges us in our attitude toward other believers and in taking the time to give of ourselves to them.

Verse: Romans 12:10

Context:

Who is speaking? Who is the audience? What is the subject? What is the time frame, beginning and ending thought?

Key Words:

In light of the definitions, how do they expand or highlight this verse for me?

Brotherly Kindness

Cross References:

Verses that support my understanding of this verse.

For Discussion:

- What is the main issue being addressed here?

- What about this verse is challenging for me to believe?

- What sinful thinking or behavior does this verse expose in me?

- What would applying this truth in my life look like?

- How can we encourage one another in the truth of this verse?

The Next Step

> To the Disciple: We cannot apply a verse like this in our own strength. We can only do it in God's strength. In humility ask Him for help.

In Hebrews 13:1, I'm told to let love of the brethren continue. How do I do this? Here are six things to work on to get you started:

1. I put other believers' interests before my own. In Romans 12:10 we learned that we are to *give preference to one another in honor*. This is an attitude commitment to sometimes set aside my agenda and take up someone else's. I say no to what I want to do and help someone else accomplish what he or she is doing. One way we do this in a conversation is to ask more questions about the other person than we spend time talking about ourselves, and then listen to what that person has to say, setting aside our "contribution."

2. Don't think too highly of yourself. In Romans 12:16 Paul shares, "Be of the same mind toward one another; do not be haughty in mind, but associate with the lowly. Do not be wise in your own estimation." If I think I'm God's gift to the world, it's hard for me to regard others before me, because frankly, I'm the best. When I see myself through God's eyes, I recognize it was not I who sought after God (Romans 3:10-12); it was He who sought after me (Romans 5:8). As this develops humility in me, I can begin to humbly regard others as more important than myself.

3. Work at being understanding to other believers' circumstances and share in their ups and downs: "Rejoice with those who rejoice, and weep with those who weep" (Romans 12:15). This takes some learning and sensitivity, so ask God for help and be patient as you grow in this. Usually this is more about your presence and understanding without saying anything than it is about you giving advice when none is solicited.

4. Regularly pray for your brothers and sisters in the Lord: "Rejoicing in hope, persevering in tribulation, devoted to prayer" (Romans 12:12). "Devoted" speaks of putting effort into learning to pray and being committed to regular times of prayer. When you pray for someone else, look for the opportunity to let them know. I once met with a

Brotherly Kindness

youth sponsor of mine who was discouraged. I told him that I had been praying for him every day for months, thinking that this announcement would encourage him. He looked at me and with a mild exhortation asked why I hadn't told him this before. He needed the encouragement of knowing that someone was praying for him.

5. Look for ways to be the answer to the prayers for your Christian family. Here, I'm connecting two ideas in Romans 12:12 & 13. Right after Paul says to be "devoted to prayer," he continues, "contributing to the needs of the saints, practicing hospitality." As you pray for a brother or sister in Christ, and especially a specific need they have, God may and often does use you to meet that need.

6. Keep looking at how Christ loves you. Remember in John 13:34 & 35 where Christ told His disciples (including us) "that you love one another, even as I have loved you, that you also love one another." At the very least this should tell me I have a lot more to grow in loving my Christian family.

One way to apply this is that as you read through the gospels, ask yourself how Christ loved the disciples and how you could take that particular example and put it into practice. An example here would be when Christ washed the disciple's feet. I can serve my wife and/or kids by fixing them a meal and doing all the clean-up, or I can help a brother with a project at his home. There are believers I can serve in specific ways. Hopefully this will get you started in growing in Brotherly Love.

What about grace?

Grace comes into play in several places here. For instance, in order to have a right and humble attitude toward oneself, one needs God's grace. Earlier in Romans 12, in verse 3, Paul writes, "For through the grace given to me I say to everyone among you not to think more highly of himself than he ought to think; but to think so as to have sound judgment."

When Paul talks about exercising our gifts in service to one another, he begins, "Since we have gifts that differ according to the grace given to us, each of us is to exercise them accordingly." God's grace helps us to rightly look at ourselves without discouragement, and also makes it possible to serve one another with the motivation of God's love.

The Next Step

Ministry Skills: "8 to 15"

In his book, Tom Mercer elaborates on the potential we have to impact our *oikos*, or households of 8 to 15: "Our households continue to be the arenas where our testimonies can have the greatest possible impact. Why is that? Because your life lived out in front of your oikos demonstrates your faith—whether you want it to or not, whether you think it does or not. We naturally have more quality opportunities to share with the people we are with most often. As a result, the faith which is demonstrated in our daily lives is more regularly scrutinized in an oikos."[2] He went on to highlight three keys to the effectiveness of witness in our households:

- Key #1: Your life sparks the interest of your oikos.
- Key #2: Your life silences the criticism of your oikos.
- Key #3: Your life establishes the validity of your message.[3]

All of this is to say that God has set you up with the relationships He has brought into your life to have an effective witness to them.

> To the Discipler: The longer you are closer to someone, the greater impact you will have on his or her life. Jesus chose 12 men to be with Him often, and during that time they were the most impacted.

Personal Worship

Few of our worship songs directly exhort us to brotherly kindness, but many that address our savior teach us by example to show brotherly kindness.

For growing in *Brotherly Kindness*, I've included these two songs:

"O To Be Like Thee"

O to be like Thee, blessed Redeemer.
This is my constant longing and prayer.
Gladly I'll forfeit all of Earth's treasures,
Jesus, Thy perfect likeness to wear.

---

2. Mercer, *8 to 15*, 96
3. Ibid. 97.

O to be like Thee. O to be like Thee,
Blessed Redeemer, pure as Thou art.
Come in Thy sweetness. Come in Thy fullness
Stamp Thine own image deep on my heart.

O to be like Thee full of compassion;
Loving, forgiving, tender and kind.
Helping the helpless. Cheering the fainting.
Seeking the wandering sinner to find.

O to be like Thee while I am pleading.
Pour out Thy Spirit. Fill with Thy love.
Make me a temple. Meet for Thy dwelling.
Fit me for life and heaven above.[4]

"Shout to the North"

Men of faith, rise up and sing
Of the great and glorious King
You are strong when you feel weak
In your brokenness complete

Shout to the north and the south
Sing to the east and the west
Jesus is Savior to all

Lord of Heaven and Earth
(Last time)
Lord of Heaven and Earth
Lord of Heaven and Earth
Lord of Heaven and Earth

Rise up women of the truth
Stand and sing to broken hearts
Who can know the healing power
Of our glorious King of love

We've been through fire
We've been through rain
We've been refined
By the power of His name

---

4. Thomas O. Chisholm, Public Domain.

The Next Step

> We've fallen deeper in love with You
> You've burned the truth on our lips
>
> Rise up church with broken wings
> Fill this place with songs again
> Of our God who reigns on high
> By His grace again we'll fly[5]

Consider This: (For Group Discussion)

1. Review your study of Romans 12:10, highlighting what God has taught you about brotherly kindness.

2. Can you think of another believer God brought into your life who encouraged you and helped you want to grow in your relationship with the Lord? How did he or she do that?

3. Which of the six suggestions given in the middle of this study seem to be the most helpful to you to grow in brotherly love?

4. How does grace impact the way we treat one another?

---

5. Martin Smith (Curios? Music UK, 1995).

Brotherly Kindness

5. What could be a modern-day example of washing someone's feet, as Jesus did with his disciples?

6. What is one way you could serve someone on your list of 8 to 15?

Chapter 14

God as Relational

What do I mean by God as Relational? By relational, I mean that God desires a relationship with us who He has created. Often when I read a list of God's attributes, I see specific character qualities that individually describe a specific characteristic. Sometimes these descriptions can seem somewhat black-and-white and academic. In describing God as relational, I am looking at many of His attributes and their application related to His desire to have a relationship with us.

After King David meditated on God being his light and salvation, David prays this prayer in Psalm 27:4, which fits well with the subject of God being relational:

> One thing I have asked from the Lord, that I shall seek: That I may dwell in the house of the Lord all the days of my life, to behold the beauty of the Lord and to meditate in His temple.

How might you rephrase this prayer to fit your situation and circumstances?

In Psalm 8, David gives us an interesting view of God and His relationship with us:

> O Lord, our Lord, how majestic is Your name in all the earth, who have displayed Your splendor above the heavens! From the mouth

God as Relational

of infants and nursing babes You have established strength because of Your adversaries, to make the enemy and the revengeful cease. When I consider Your heavens, the work of Your fingers, the moon and the stars, which You have ordained; what is man that Your take thought of him, and the son of man that You care for him? Yet You have made him a little lower than God, and You crown him with glory and majesty. You make him to rule over the works of Your hands; You have put all things under his feet, all sheep and oxen, and also the beasts of the field, the birds of the heavens and the fish of the sea, whatever passes through the paths of the seas. O Lord, our Lord, how majestic is Your name in all the earth!

- Have you ever taken the time to marvel at the thought that David is expressing here?

- What does this tell you about God?

> To the Disciple: Think of a daily quiet time as an opportunity to daily "behold the beauty of the Lord and to meditate in His temple." We are His temple, so whenever we stop to meditate on the Lord, this is true.

Next, copy Hebrews 4:16 onto a 3-by-5 card for your next verse to memorize and study in the verse study section. Take a few minutes to review your other verses. As you review, ask God to show you what each verse means and how it relates to your life this day.

> To the Discipler: Now is the time to persevere in getting to know those who meet with you. Always ask questions to learn more about them. By doing this, you will always be personalizing the study to their lives.

The Next Step

Journaling

Go to the Journaling section and write down something God has taught you in this lesson so far and respond to God with a prayer.

Verse Study

Study Hebrews 4:16, asking God to show you how to draw near to Him. Stop and thank Him for such an amazing privilege.

Verse: Hebrews 4:16

Context:

Who is speaking? Who is the audience? What is the subject? What is the time frame, beginning and ending thought?

Key Words:

In light of the definitions, how do they expand or highlight this verse for me?

Cross References:

Verses that support my understanding of this verse.

For Discussion:

- What is the main issue being addressed here?

- What about this verse is challenging for me to believe?

- What sinful thinking or behavior does this verse expose in me?

- What would applying this truth in my life look like?

- How can we encourage one another in the truth of this verse?

Many of God's attributes are relational in nature. His love, mercy, compassion, goodness, grace, patience, and even His wrath and jealousy have their meanings in relationships. When we look at God's love and compassion we see those expressed in sending His Son to be our savior so that we might live with Him forever. We speak of the incarnation of Christ, which literally means "in the flesh."

Paul addresses the incarnation of Christ in Philippians 2:6–8:

The Next Step

> For He, who had always been God by nature, did not cling to his prerogatives as God's equal, but stripped himself of all privilege by consenting to be a slave by nature and being born as mortal man. And, having become a man, He humbled Himself by living a life of utter obedience, even to the extent of dying and the death he died was the death of a common criminal. (Phillips version)

John speaks of Christ's incarnation in John 1:14: "And the Word became flesh, and dwelt among us, and we say His glory, glory as of the only begotten from the Father, full of grace and truth." Several times in the Bible, our Christian life is described as "our walk," or our "dwelling with Christ." These phrases speak of living with someone, of living life together.

Paul in 2 Corinthians 8:9 writes, "For you know the grace of our Lord Jesus Christ, that though He was rich, yet for your sake He became poor, so that you through His poverty might become rich."

I ask the question: Why did God do this? Why did Christ become a man and die? Was it just that we might have eternal life? I would say that part of the reason was that we would dwell with Him forever. In John 13:36, Peter asks Christ where He is going. Christ responds, "Where I go, you cannot follow Me now; but you will follow later." Three verses later Christ shares this with His disciples:

> Do not let you heart be troubled; believe in God believe also in Me. In My Father's house are many dwelling places; if it were not so, I would have told you; for I go to prepare a place for you. If I go and prepare a place for you, I will come again and receive you to Myself, that where I am, there you may be also. (John 14:1–3)

We call the Bible the revelation of God because He gave it to us to more fully communicate about Himself. In the very beginning of the book of Hebrews we read, "God, after He spoke long ago to the fathers in the prophets in many portions and in many ways, in these last days has spoken to us in His son." Several times in Hebrews and also in James we are told to draw near to God and He will draw near to us. In these passages we see a relational God.

In this discussion it is important that we recognize that God needs nothing. His desire for us to dwell with Him comes from His heart, not from a need. God's perfection is defined as follows: "God completely possesses all excellent qualities and lacks no part of any qualities that would be desirable for Him."[1] He is perfect (Matthew 5:48) and lacks nothing. In Job

---

1. Grudem, *Systematic Theology*, 218.

38, the Lord begins a reply to Job, asking Him, "Where were you when I laid the foundation of the earth?" He goes on to imply that Job was not needed for any part of what God has done in all of creation. Job begins his answer in 40:4 with "Behold, I am insignificant; what can I reply to you? I lay my hand on my mouth."

What I find amazing is that, on one hand, God does not need us to be perfect in any way, yet He desires that we walk with Him and know Him and that we look forward to spending eternity with Him, and that He desires to reveal more of Himself to us (John 14:21).

One of the implications of the title *The Next Step* is that I've trusted in Christ as my savior, so, what's the next step? I'm not just referring to your and my next task, but what is the next step in my relationship with God? How do I walk with Him as Enoch did? How do I grow as a friend of God, as Abraham was called? How can I become a man or woman after God's own heart as David was?

What are the implications to us of God being relational?

1. Understanding God as relational provides the greatest motivation and example for us to grow in Brotherly Love for one another.

2. Understanding God as relational reminds me that a daily walk with God is not a task to be accomplished but a relationship in which to grow.

3. When I understand God's desire to reveal Himself to me (John 14:21), my reading and meditating on the scripture is a great adventure to discover more about God.

4. To respond to a world that thinks God is at a distance. He is not at a distance. He has come to us.

5. I begin to better understand the purpose of man: To glorify God and enjoy Him forever.

> To the Disciple: Are you getting to know God better? Are you growing in your relationship with God? Do you talk with Him often and listen to Him even more? We listen to Him every time we read and meditate on His Word, the Bible.

The Next Step

What about grace?

Grace comes into play when I think of an infinite God reaching out to someone insignificant like me. That He would prepare a place for me, that His son became a man and then took on my sin so that I could spend eternity with Him makes no sense apart from the grace and love of God.

Ministry Skills: "8 to 15"

When I pray for the 8 to 15 people God has supernaturally brought into my life, I am not praying that they will join my church or even change their religion or lives, except as it relates to a relationship with God. If they haven't trusted in what Christ did on the cross as their substitute, they cannot know God. By trusting in Christ as his or her substitute and savior, we can be reconciled to God and an eternal relationship begins. That is what I pray for each person on my list: to know God and Jesus Christ whom He has sent. Take a few minutes and pray for those *God has brought into your life* right now.

> To the Disciple: Every attribute of God is exercised and satisfied in the work of Christ on the cross.

> To the Discipler: Ask God to show you illustrations from your own life to model the specifics from each week's lessons. A good illustration connects God's truths with our hearts.

Personal Worship

Here are two songs that could help you meditate on God as relational. As I sing a worship song or meditate on one of the Psalms (the Old Testament songbook), I often have to pray a song's phrases, because while I know they are not true in me yet, I want them to be.

Feel free to carry this book with you during the day, as you might have some free time to quietly sing and reflect on our great God and pray through these songs.

"Amazing Love"

I'm forgiven because You were forsaken,
I'm accepted, You were condemned.
I am alive and well, Your spirit is within me,
Because You died and rose again.
(Repeat x2)

(Chorus)
Amazing love,
How can it be
That You, my King, should die for me?
Amazing love,
I know it's true.
It's my joy to honor You,
In all I do, I honor You.

I'm forgiven because You were forsaken,
I'm accepted, You were condemned.
I am alive and well, Your spirit is within me,
Because You died and rose again.

(Repeat chorus x2)

You are my King
Jesus You are my King[2]

"Whom Shall I Fear"

You hear me when I call
You are my morning song
Though darkness fills the night
It cannot hide the light
Whom shall I fear?

You crush the enemy
Underneath my feet
You are my sword and shield
Though trouble linger still
Whom shall I fear?

---

2. Billy James Foote (worshiptogether.com Songs, 1999).

The Next Step

> I know who goes before me
> I know who stands behind
> The God of angel armies is always by my side
> The One who reigns forever
> He is a friend of mine
> The God of angel armies is always by my side
>
> My strength is in Your name
> For You alone can save
> You will deliver me
> Yours is the victory
> Whom shall I fear?
> Whom shall I fear?
>
> And nothing formed against me shall stand
> You hold the whole world in Your hands
> I'm holding onto Your promises
> You are faithful
> You are faithful[3]

Consider This: (For Group Discussion)

1. How would you describe King David's relationship with the Lord?

2. Who else in the Bible seemed to have a close relationship with the Lord? How is that shown in the Bible?

3. Review the study of Hebrews 4:16, sharing what God has taught you from this verse.

---

3. Chris Tomlin, Ed Cash, Scott Cash (Worship Together Music, Sixsteps Songs, A Thousand Generations Publ., 2013).

God as Relational

4. What did you learn about God from this study? Were you reminded of something you might have forgotten about Him?

5. What can you do this week to spend more time with the Lord, to grow in your relationship with Him?

6. Review the worship songs at the end of this chapter and pick out a line that is especially meaningful to you as a result of doing this study.

Chapter 15

Love

The *seventh* and final *virtue* is *love*. This is *agape* love, the love of Christ, a sacrificial love. The word for love here is *agape*, in contrast to *phileo* (brotherly love), or *eros* (physical or sexual love). *Agape* is defined as love (primarily of Christian love), deep concern and interest in another.

"Agape is the queen of the virtues and denotes self-sacrificing action in behalf of another."[1] Philippians 2:3–7 wonderfully illustrates what this kind of love looks like:

> Do nothing from selfishness or empty conceit, but with humility of mind regard one another as more important than yourselves; do not merely look out for your own personal interests, but also for the interests of others. Have this attitude in yourselves which was also in Christ Jesus, who, although He existed in the form of God, did not regard equality with God a thing to be grasped, but emptied Himself, taking the form of a bond-servant, and being made in the likeness of men.

An interesting verse that bridges brotherly love and agape love is I Peter 1:22: "Since you have in obedience to the truth purified your souls for a sincere love of the brethren, fervently love one another from the heart."

Start your time with the Lord in prayer, looking at Paul's prayer for the Philippians in Philippians 1:9–11:

> And this I pray, that your love may abound still more and more in real knowledge and all discernment, so that you may approve the

---

1. Gaebelein, *The Expositor's Bible Commentary*, 270.

things that are excellent, in order to be sincere and blameless until the day of Christ; having been filled with the fruit of righteousness which comes through Jesus Christ, to the glory and praise of God.

- I find this is a very helpful prayer as I desire to grow in a particular area or if I am faced with an important decision.
- This is a great prayer to pray for our love to grow.
- This is also a great prayer to pray for our children, as we know they will be faced with many decisions.

> To the Disciple: My growth in any area begins when I come to the Lord and say, "Lord, I do not have this quality in my life. I need your help to grow in this." This is especially true with love.

In speaking to the children of Israel through Jeremiah the prophet, God told Israel in Jeremiah 31:3, "I have loved you with an everlasting love; therefore I have drawn you with lovingkindness."

Later, in the New Testament, John probably had this verse in mind as he wrote:

> Beloved, let us love one another, for love is from God; and everyone who loves is born of God and knows God. The one who does not love does not know God, for God is love. By this the love of God was manifested in us, that God has sent His only begotten Son into the world so that we might live through Him. In this is love, not that we loved God, but that He loved us and sent His Son to be the propitiation for our sins. Beloved, if God so loved us, we also ought to love one another." (I John 4:7-11)

- Here's a roundabout way to look at God's love for you: If God were a person like you or me, why would He have a hard time loving you?

The Next Step

- Now reflect on the fact that God is not like us, and in spite of how we might respond, God did love you with an everlasting love and He drew you to Himself with His lovingkindness.

Next, copy John 13:34 & 35 onto a 3-by-5 card for your next verse to memorize and study in the verse study section. Sometimes I'll just read through my memory verses, looking over each card and thinking about what they mean. This is still a way to review your verses and keep them at the front of your thoughts.

> To the Discipler: Mix up how you help those you meet with in their scripture memory. This week ask them to share with you one of the verses that has been especially encouraging to them in this study.

Journaling

Go to the end of this book and write down in the Journaling section something God has taught you in this lesson so far and respond to God with a prayer.

Verse Study

In John 13:34 & 35, Christ speaks of loving one another as a new commandment. As you study this verse, think through how this is new.

Love

Verse: John 13:34, 35

Context:

Who is speaking? Who is the audience? What is the subject? What is the time frame, beginning and ending thought?

Key Words:

In light of the definitions, how do they expand or highlight this verse for me?

Cross References:

Verses that support my understanding of this verse.

For Discussion:

- What is the main issue being addressed here?

The Next Step

- What about this verse is challenging for me to believe?

- What sinful thinking or behavior does this verse expose in me?

- What would applying this truth in my life look like?

- How can we encourage one another in the truth of this verse?

> To the Disciple: People around us are especially watching to see how we handle difficult circumstances. Those are probably our greatest times of testimony.

When we think of love we often reflect on I Corinthians 13, especially verse 4 and following. This is a great place to start in our definition of Christian love:

> Love is patient, love is kind and is not jealous; love does not brag and is not arrogant, does not act unbecomingly; it does not seek its own, is not provoked, does not take into account a wrong suffered, does not rejoice in unrighteousness, but rejoices with the truth; bears all things, believes all things, hopes all things, endures all things." (1 Corinthians 13:4–7)

So one aspect of growing in our love — supplying love to our brotherly kindness — is putting these verses into practice. Here are some examples of what each looks like. This is part of a message I share at weddings to help new couples begin to grow in love for one another:

"*'Love is patient'* tells me that I will let my spouse grow at his or her pace and I won't insist that he or she does it my way now." With my brothers and sisters in Christ I will be patient as I listen and in allowing them to grow as God works in them.

"*'Love is kind'* tells me that I need to be gentle and think about how what I am saying or doing comes across to the other person." With others, I will respond with kind words and not be harsh or sarcastic in my responses.

"*'Love is not jealous'* encourages me to trust my mate's faithfulness to me and not to insist that I always have all his or her attention." As I see what other believers have or what they are doing for the Lord, I will not envy their possessions or skills, but praise the Lord for them and be quick to encourage them in these areas.

"*'Love does not brag and is not arrogant'* means that I will value my husband's or wife's desires above my own and will listen to them more that I talk." This really addresses the tongue. As I am around others, I will look for opportunities to ask questions and not be so quick to talk about myself. I will look for ways to build up others more than to build up myself.

"*'Does not seek its own'* challenges me to put my husband's or wife's desires above mine and to be a servant to him or her." This should cause me to ask often how I can serve others God has put in my life. This will take some of my time to think about what they need, and also about how and when I can serve them, and then meet their needs before my own.

"*'Is not provoked and does not take into account a wrong suffered'* means that my husband or wife can do something that would normally offend, but I will not be offended. I will not bring up any past mistakes or disagreements." How often other believers offend me. I will work on not being offended. Instead I will bring the person to the Lord in prayer, and I will remind myself of all that the Lord has forgiven me. Ephesians 4:32 is so important here.

Another aspect of applying and growing in love is in setting aside an agenda, with its time constraints, and giving time to others, and laying aside my preferences and personal schedule and giving to others. 1 Corinthians 13:5 begins to address this in the phrase, "does not seek its own." Philippians 2:3–4 guides me here where Paul writes:

> Do nothing from selfishness or empty conceit, but with humility of mind regard one another as more important than yourselves; do not merely look out for your own personal interests, but also for the interests of others.

Our time is possibly the most valuable commodity we have. It definitely costs me to set aside my agenda or schedule and give my time to help another. As Paul points out, I begin changing my attitude by having "humility of mind." My understanding about this is that I recognize my own weakness and inability to grow in love and be unselfish apart from God's work in me. Then I will consciously decide to make that other person more important than me. My next actions will support that.

What about grace?

We need God's grace to be able to give grace to another. He is the reservoir we must draw from, our source of every good thing. Paul spells this out in 2 Corinthians 9:8: "And God is able to make all grace abound to you, so that always having all sufficiency in everything, you may have an abundance for every good deed."

Ministry Skills: "8 to 15"

Let me give you an extra assignment this week to help you engage with some of your 8 to 15. Pick someone on your list and learn five new things about him or her this week. Don't talk about yourself or your interests. Your whole goal is to focus on him or her. Use good follow-up questions to learn even more and become more interested. As you do, ask God to give you a genuine interest and love for that person.

> To the Discipler: If you haven't already, visit those you meet with in their homes and survey their surroundings to learn more about them. People put out on display hints at what they find important.

Personal Worship

For growing in *Love*, I've included these two songs:

"The Heart of Worship"

When the music fades and all is stripped away
And I simply come
Longing just to bring something that's of worth
That will bless Your heart

I'll bring You more than a song
For a song in itself is not what You have required
You search much deeper within
Through the way things appear
You're looking into my heart

I'm coming back to the heart of worship
And it's all about You, it's all about You Jesus
I'm sorry Lord for the things I've made it
And it's all about You, it's all about You Jesus

King of endless worth no one could express
How much You deserve
Though I'm weak and poor all I have is Yours
Every single breath[2]

"I Could Sing of Your Love Forever"

Over the mountains and the sea
Your river runs with love for me
And I will open up my heart
And let the healer set me free
I'm happy to be in the truth
And I will daily lift my hands
For I will always sing of when your love came down

I could sing of your love forever

Over the mountains and the sea
Your river runs with love for me
And I will open up my heart
And let the healer set me free
I'm happy to be in truth
And I will daily lift my hands
For I will always sing of when your love came down

---

2. Matt Redman (Thankyou Music, 1999).

The Next Step

> I could sing of your love forever (8x)
>
> Oh I feel like dancing
> It's foolishness I know
> But when the world has seen the light
> They will dance with joy
> Like we're dancing now
> I could sing of your love forever (8x)[3]

Consider This: (For Group Discussion)

1. Thinking through all seven virtues, why did Peter end with Love? How is love the culmination of the other six virtues?

2. Review your study of John 13:34 and 35 and share what you learned about growing in "love."

3. Pick one of the phrases in I Corinthians 13:4–7 and expand on how you can apply it this week.

4. What is an interest of someone else's you can put before your own this week, and how will you do this?

---

3. Martin Smith (Curious? Music UK, 1994).

Love

5. How can we apply this thought in our relationship with God (putting His interests before my own)?

6. Set aside some time (maybe make an appointment) to meet with God and meditate on and sing or pray one of the worship songs to God.

Chapter 16

The Love of God

This week's verse to memorize and meditate on is 1 John 4:10: "In this is love, not that we loved God, but that He loved us and sent His son to be the propitiation for our sins." The pinnacle of virtues we are to add to our faith is love, and the supreme source to learn about this love is God "who loved us."

This week, let's begin by meditating on the first verse of "And Can It Be."

> And can it be that I should gain
> an interest in the Savior's blood!
> Died he for me, who caused his pain!
> For me, who him to death pursued?
> Amazing love! How can it be
> that thou, my God, shouldst die for me?
> Amazing love! How can it be
> that thou, my God, shouldst die for me?[1]

In Ephesians 3:14–19, Paul gives us a great prayer to pray regarding growing in our understanding about God's love.

> For this reason I bow my knees before the Father, from whom every family in heaven and on earth derives its name, that He would grant you, according to the riches of His glory, to be strengthened with power through His Spirit in the inner man, so that Christ may dwell in your hearts through faith; and that you, being rooted and grounded in love, may be able to comprehend with all the

---

1. Charles Wesley, Public Domain.

saints what is the breadth and length and height and depth, and to know the love of Christ which surpasses knowledge, that you may be filled up to all the fullness of God.

What can you take from this prayer in your beginning prayer today?

In our second lesson we memorized Lamentations 3:22 and 23. The topic was God's faithfulness, but do you remember how this verse on God's faithfulness began? (I'm sure you do, as you memorized it.)

"The Lord's lovingkindnesses indeed never cease, for His compassions never fail. They are new every morning; great is Your faithfulness."

- How is God's love and faithfulness connected in these verses?

- What does this tell you about God?

> To the Disciple: In the same way that space and time are infinite, God's attributes are infinite in Him. As His existence is eternal so His love is without measure.

Next, copy 1 John 4:10 onto a 3-by-5 card for your next verse to memorize and study in the verse study section. Take a few minutes now to review your other verses. Take at least one of your memory verses each morning to think about from a prayer point of view and pray for that verse to be true or clear in your life today.

The Next Step

> To the Discipler: As you finish this study, ask those who are meeting with you which prayer from the beginning of each chapter they would most like to be prayed for them. Then commit to pray that prayer for them on a regular basis as you finish.

Journaling

Go to the Journaling section in the back of this book and write down something God has taught you in this lesson so far and respond to God with a prayer.

Verse Study

Study 1 John 4:10, asking God to show you some of the depths of His love. Stop and thank God for such an amazing love.

Verse: I John 4:10

Context: (Who is speaking? Who is the audience? What is the subject? What is the time frame, beginning and ending thought?)

Key Words:

In light of the definitions, how do they expand or highlight this verse for me?

Cross References: (Verses that support my understanding of this verse)

The Love of God

For Discussion:

- What is the main issue being addressed here?

- What about this verse is challenging for me to believe?

- What sinful thinking or behavior does this verse expose in me?

- What would applying this truth in my life look like?

- How can we encourage one another in the truth of this verse?

"God's love means that God eternally gives of himself to others. This definition understands love as self-giving for the benefit of others. This attribute of God shows that it is part of his nature to give of himself in order to bring about blessing or good to others."[2] Below are a few truths about God's love. I hope they will launch you on a lifelong quest to explore the depths of God's love.

---

2. Grudem, *Systematic Theology*, 198.

A. *God teaches us about love by demonstrating His love to us.* "By this the love of God was manifested in us that God has sent His only begotten Son into the world so that we might live through Him. In this is love, not that we loved God, but that He loved us and sent His Son to be the propitiation for our sins." (I John 4:9-10) This tells me that love can be seen in someone's actions. God showed us what love looked like by sending His son to leave heaven and live as a man and die on a cross. This showed us what His love looked like, but it also impacted us personally, as we are the direct recipients of this demonstration.

B. *God's demonstration of His love was to personally sacrifice His son.* "For God so loved the world that He gave His only begotten Son, that whoever believes in Him shall not perish, but have eternal life. For God did not send the Son into the world to judge the world, but that the world might be saved through Him." (John 3:16, 17) I add this here because it can be easy to downplay God's sacrificial gift, knowing Christ would rise from the dead. I do not fully understand God's sacrifice, but I know it was much greater than just sending His son away for a while and then getting Him back. 2 Corinthians 5:21 helps some to begin to understand Christ's sacrifice. This really was a costly gift.

C. *God's love is never ending. It will never run out.* "The Lord's lovingkindnesses indeed never ceases, for His compassions never fail. They are new every morning; great is Your faithfulness" (Lamentations 3:22,23). Along that line, Paul's prayer in Ephesians 3:14-19 implies that God's love is greater than our ability to measure. One implication from this is that He always has more love to give us. What ever I might do wrong, I can come back to Him. When we look out at the people who live around us, no one is beyond God's love and grace.

D. *Love and fellowship with God and knowing God more and more all go hand in hand.* In 1 John 4:16 we read "We have come to know and have believed the love which God has for us. God is love, and the one who abides in love abides in God, and God abides in him." This verse brings together God's love and our response to love Him back, and as this happens, we are abiding in Him. The Psalmist understood this in Psalm 73:28 when he stated, "But as for me, the nearness of God is my good."

The implication here is that God desires a close relationship with us and I can trust in James' invitation, "Draw near to God and He will draw near to you."

The Love of God

I also connect God's love, and fellowship with God, with getting to know Him better. There is an amazing promise at the end of John 14:21: "He who has My commandments and keeps them is the one who loves Me; and he who loves Me will be loved by My Father, and I will love him and will disclose Myself to him." When God loves us, He manifests Himself to us. He shows us more of who He is. That motivates me to spend more and more time with Him.

> To the Disciple: Never hesitate to ask God to show you His love by asking for forgiveness, grace, mercy, or encouragement.

What about grace?

To show how much love God has and how well His love responds to sin, Paul tells us in Romans 5:20 & 21, "The Law came in so that the transgression would increase; but where sin increased, grace abounded all the more, so that, as sin reigned in death, even so grace would reign through righteousness to eternal life through Jesus Christ our Lord."

Ministry Skills: "8 to 15"

The goal of introducing "8 to 15" in this study is not to just give you a 16-week ministry focus along with this study but to start you on a lifelong ministry of seeing God's hand at bringing people into your life for you to pray for, get to know, and, as you engage with them, see God use you in their lives. God is changing the world, and part of His plan to change people for eternity involves you.

> To the Disciple: When we think of whom to put on our list of 8 to 15, let the capacity of God's love, not your capacity to love, determine who to include.

> To the Discipler: Work at instilling within those you are discipling God's desire to use them to share this material with others. Being faithful means being faithful to give this to someone else.

The Next Step

Personal Worship

Here are two songs that will help you meditate on God's love. Feel free to carry this book with you during the day as you might have some free time to quietly sing and reflect on our great God. Add more worship songs to those in this book as God encourages you in your times of worship.

"My Savior's Love"

I stand amazed in the presence
Of Jesus the Nazarene,
And wonder how He could love me,
A sinner, condemned, unclean.

Oh, how marvelous! Oh, how wonderful!
And my song shall ever be:
Oh, how marvelous! Oh, how wonderful!
Is my Savior's love for me!

For me it was in the garden
He prayed: "Not My will, but Thine."
He had no tears for His own griefs,
But sweat drops of blood for mine.

In pity angels beheld Him,
And came from the world of light
To comfort Him in the sorrows
He bore for my soul that night.

He took my sins and my sorrows,
He made them His very own;
He bore the burden to Calv'ry,
And suffered and died alone.

When with the ransomed in glory
His face I at last shall see,
'Twill be my joy through the ages
To sing of His love for me.[3]

---

3. Charles H. Gabriel, Public Domain.

The Love of God

"Your Love Never Fails"

Higher than the mountains that I face
Stronger than the power of the grave
Constant through the trial and the change
One thing remains
One thing remains

Your love never fails it never gives up it never runs out on me x3

On and on and on and on it goes
It overwhelms and satisfies my soul
And I never ever have to be afraid
One thing remains

In death and in life I'm confident and covered by the power of your great love
My debt is paid there's nothing that can separate my heart from your great love[4]

Consider This: (For Group Discussion)

1. What circumstances did God use in your life to help you first begin to understand that He loves you?

2. Share what you learned in your study of I John 4:10?

3. How has God shown you more about Himself as you've spent time with Him in His word?

---

4. Matt Redman (Thankyou Music, 1999).

The Next Step

4. What is the most helpful truth you learned in this chapter?

5. How has studying God's grace in every chapter impacted you?

Journaling

When using a journal in my daily devotions, I have found the following format helpful:

> Date:
> Scripture verses:
> This morning I learned:
> Lord, help me today to: .

- I like to personalize what I'm reading. It helps me think through how to practically apply this scripture to my life.
- I will read as much as I need to take something with me from God's word. Sometimes this may be only a few verses. Other times this may be a whole chapter.
- Don't feel bad if you skip a day. Just pick it up again the next day.
- Try to find a regular place and time to do this every day.

I've tried to provide you with a fairly open and flexible format for journaling in this workbook. You can journal daily as God is teaching you, or weekly. Use this tool as much as possible in this study to see its full potential. One result of journaling is that after a period of time you can look back over what God has been teaching you and often see a particular area He's working on in your life. You can also see an area that you are growing in to encourage you.

Writing is often overlooked as a ministry skill, yet we have much of the New Testament because of believers who wrote down what God was teaching them. Who knows, God may use you through your writing to encourage other believers.

Date:
Scripture verses:
This morning I learned:

Lord, help me today to:

Date:
Scripture verses:
This morning I learned:

Lord, help me today to:

Date:
Scripture verses:
This morning I learned:

Lord, help me today to:

Journaling

Date:
Scripture verses:
This morning I learned:

Lord, help me today to:

Date:
Scripture verses:
This morning I learned:

Lord, help me today to:

Date:
Scripture verses:
This morning I learned:

Lord, help me today to:

The Next Step

Date:
Scripture verses:
This morning I learned:

Lord, help me today to:

Date:
Scripture verses:
This morning I learned:

Lord, help me today to:

Date:
Scripture verses:
This morning I learned:

Lord, help me today to:

Journaling

Date:
Scripture verses:
This morning I learned:

Lord, help me today to:

Date:
Scripture verses:
This morning I learned:

Lord, help me today to:

Date:
Scripture verses:
This morning I learned:

Lord, help me today to:

Bibliography

Blum, Edwin A. and Gaebelein, Frank E. *The Expositor's Bible Commentary.* Zondervan Publishing House, 1981.
Bridges, Jerry. *The Pursuit of Holiness.* Navpress, 1984.
Brown, Colin. *The New International Dictionary of New Testament Theology Vol. 3.* 4th printing. Zondervan Publishing House, 1979.
Cole, Steve. "The Priority of True Worship." Message given at Flagstaff Christian Fellowship, August 11, 2013.
Green, Michael, and Professor R. V. G Tasker.. *Tyndale New Testament Commentaries: The Second Epistle of Peter and the Epistle of Jude.* Wm. B. Eerdmans Publishing Company, 1976.
Grenz, Stanley J., et al. *Pocket Dictionary of Theological Terms.* InterVarsity Press, 1999.
Grudem, Wayne. *Systematic Theology.* Zondervan Publishing House, 1994.
Kennedy, James. "Do You Know" gospel tract. Evangelism Explosion, 1997.
Lenski, Dr. Richard C.H. *The Interpretation of I and II Epistles of Peter, the Three Epistles of John, and the Epistle of Jude.* Augsburg Publishing House, 1966.
MacArthur, John. *The MacArthur Study Bible.* Word Bibles, 1997.
Marshall, Colin and Tony Payne. *The Trellis and the Vine.* Matthias Media, 2009.
Mercer, Tom. *8 to 15: The World Is Smaller Than You Think.* Oikos Books, 2009.
Morely, Patrick. *No Man Left Behind.* Moody Publishers, 2006.
Packer, J.I. *Evangelism and the Sovereignty of God.* InterVarsity Press, 1991.
Piper, John. *Desiring God.* Multnomah Books, 1986.
Robertson, Archibald Thomas. *Word Pictures in the New Testament.* Broadman Press, 1933.
Sloan, John. "Forums of Four," 2000.
Strong, James. *Strong's Exhaustive Concordance of the Bible.* Mac Donald Publishing Company.
Vine, W.E., et al. *Vine's Complete Expository Dictionary of Old and New Testament Words.* Thomas Nelson Publishers, 1961, 1970.

www.ingramcontent.com/pod-product-compliance
Lightning Source LLC
Chambersburg PA
CBHW050808160426
43192CB00010B/1680